the garlic companion

the garlic companion

RECITES, CRAFTS,
PRESERVATION TECHNIQUES,
and SIMPLE WAYS TO
GROW YOUR OWN

KRISTIN GRAVES

PHOTOGRAPHY BY MICHAEL PIAZZA
AND DONG KIM

Storey Publishing

*The mission of Storey Publishing is to serve our customers by
publishing practical information that encourages
personal independence in harmony with the environment.*

EDITED BY Carleen Madigan, Kelly Smith Trimble,
and Sarah Guare Slattery

ART DIRECTION AND BOOK DESIGN BY
Carolyn Eckert

TEXT PRODUCTION BY Jennifer Jepson Smith

COVER PHOTOGRAPHY BY © Michael Piazza
Photography/SAINT LUCY Represents, except
© Dong Kim, back t.r.

INTERIOR PHOTOGRAPHY BY
© Dong Kim, 8 t.l. & m.r., 11 m.r. & b.r., 14–15, 31 m.r.,
40–41, 62, 69 b.r., 119 m.r. & b.r., 129, 131, 137 t.l.
& b.r., 144–146, 147 t.l. & b.l., 154–162, 165, 169, 171,
175, 181, 185–187, 189–190, 192, 195, 197 b.r., 198,
199 t. & m., 200, 203, 208–209, 211 t. & m., 213,
214 r. & l.m.;

© Michael Piazza Photography/SAINT LUCY
Represents, facing title page, 1–6, 8 b.r. & l. & t.r., 11
t.l. & t.r., 12, 17, 21, 23, 25–26, 29, 32, 33 t., 34, 37–39,
42–50, 53–56, 59–60, 63, 65–66, 69 all but b.r., 70,
73, 75–76, 79–80, 83, 85–86, 89–90, 93–94, 97–98,
101–102, 105, 107–109, 111–112, 115–116, 119 t.r. &
l., 120, 123–127, 132–133, 135–136, 137 t.r., 138–139,
141–143, 147 r., 148–149, 167, 172–174, 177–179, 183,
197 all but b.r., 205–207, 210, 214 b.l. & t.l., 216,
224, 225

ADDITIONAL PHOTOGRAPHY BY Annie Spratt/
Unsplash, 150; Antonio Tempesta/The Elisha
Whittelsey Collection, The Elisha Whittelsey
Fund, 1951, Metropolian Museum of Art/CC0 1.0
Universal Public Domain Dedication/Wikimedia
Commons, 19 l.; Courtesy of Kristin Graves,
11 b.l., 33 b., 64, 168, 191; Helgi Halldórsson from
Reykjavík, Iceland/CC BY-SA 2.0/Wikimedia
Commons, 20; © Julian Eales/Alamy Stock Photo,
31 t.l.; © Kevin Schafer/Alamy Stock Photo, 31
b.l.; Marianne Stokes/Public domain/Wikimedia
Commons, 19 b.r.; © Mariusz Jurgielewicz/
Alamy Stock Photo, 31 t.r.; Mars Vilaubi © Storey
Publishing, 19 t.r., 151–153, 199 b.; Pierre André
Leclercq/CC BY-SA 4.0/Wikimedia Commons,
31 b.r.; Tijana Drndarski/Unsplash, 211 b.

FOOD STYLING BY Catrine Kelty

ADDITIONAL STYLING BY Kristin Graves and
Michael Piazza

TEXT © 2024 by Kristin Graves

Storey books may be purchased in bulk for business,
educational, or promotional use. Special editions or
book excerpts can also be created to specification.
For details, please contact your local bookseller
or the Hachette Book Group Special Markets
Department at special.markets@hbgusa.com.

STOREY PUBLISHING
210 MASS MoCA Way
North Adams, MA 01247
storey.com

Storey Publishing is an imprint of Workman
Publishing, a division of Hachette Book Group, Inc.,
1290 Avenue of the Americas, New York, NY 10104.
The Storey Publishing name and logo are registered
trademarks of Hachette Book Group, Inc.

ISBNs: 978-1-63586-686-5 (hardcover);
978-1-63586-687-2 (ebook)

Printed in China through Asia Pacific Offset
10 9 8 7 6 5 4 3 2 1

Library of Congress Cataloging-in-Publication Data
on file

*To my dear friend Nikola,
without whom I would have never
found the courage to try*

CONTENTS

Preface

GARLIC! If you're reading this book, you probably love it as much as I do. Or maybe you've become intrigued by garlic and want to know more. Garlic is bold, tenacious, and full of warmth. It's well known for adding the perfect spicy flavor to everything from pasta and pizza to hummus and pesto. It can also enhance the sumptuousness of a rich and creamy butter, bring out the essence of other ingredients when combined with a sprinkling of salt, or boost the sweetness of a drizzle of a fragrant floral honey.

There's no shortage of spices to elevate a dining experience, but garlic's culinary versatility is truly impressive. It can be a stand-alone flavor bomb, making a big impact, or serve as a subtle companion that draws out the more daring attributes of a recipe's other elements. The cloves found within a garlic bulb contain slightly sweet characteristics that contrast with the fiery flavor for which they're widely known.

It's also a beautiful and unique plant and one that brings people together!

Over the past 100 years, the fields on my family's farm in Alberta, Canada, have been green pastures for cattle or vast acres of cereal grains, and they are now home to 75,000 bulbs of garlic.

My sister, Erica, and I are the fifth generation to call the farm home. I was a radiology technician working in trauma until a particularly harrowing case made me reconsider my career. I turned back to the farm and the land to heal. There I began growing 60 different varieties of vegetables and herbs for a CSA (community-supported agriculture) program that I called Fifth Gen. Looking for a way to generate year-round income for the operation, I became curious about methods to extend the seasons for local food. I had also just harvested my first-ever crop of garlic and could not believe how amazing it tasted.

It was there that a new dream started to take shape: a sustainable future for our farm, with the implementation of greener growing practices, centered around garlic.

Garlic is bold, tenacious, and full of warmth. It's well known for adding the perfect spicy flavor to everything.

The cultivation of heirloom varieties connected me to the knowledge that I am part of something so much bigger than myself.

What began as a mild curiosity quickly became so much more, as my eyes were opened to the vast history, uses, health benefits, and intriguing lore surrounding garlic. I can tell you from experience that the fascination goes even deeper when you grow juicy garlic bulbs in the neat and tidy rows of a garden. The cultivation of heirloom varieties connected me to the knowledge that I am part of something so much bigger than myself, not to mention the many mental and emotional health benefits that come from tending a garden full of healthful and useful ingredients to stock the kitchen pantry.

Almost instantly with my first garlic harvest, the wheels in my head started turning as I tried to think of delicious concoctions that were garlic forward. The first was a smoked garlic bulb. When I shared the idea with my dad, asking if he thought it was even possible, his exact answer was, "I can smoke anything."

From there he and I teamed up to merge his lifetime of experience in farming with my knowledge of small-scale growing and love of culinary creativity. What my dad knows about agriculture is what his father taught him, and what his father taught him, and so on. But for the first time in five generations, that knowledge is being passed down from father to daughter, something for which I am unbelievably proud.

Did I dream of becoming a garlic farmer? The truth is, no. I was raised with an understanding of where our food comes from and a deep appreciation for the people who produce it, but I envisioned a very different future for myself. Sometimes life has other plans.

I cherish the wealth of knowledge I have amassed from years spent working in the field. My love for garlic has only deepened as our farm's crop doubles in size time and time again. I hope to ignite that same enthusiasm in you through recipes featuring fun, new methods of cooking with garlic; gardening advice for those who want to grow their own; and more ideas for sharing the beauty of garlic with family and friends. I invite you to join me on this journey!

Growing garlic on our family's land is my commitment toward the future, building something for the generations to come.

1

KNOW AND LOVE

the wonderful world of garlic

Garlic is an allium (*Allium sativum*, to be exact), part of the lily family and cousin to onions, shallots, and leeks. Though most people view the fragrant bulb as an herb, garlic is technically a root vegetable. It's one of the few vegetables used more as a flavoring than as the main focus in a dish. Due to its pungent aroma, garlic is sometimes referred to as the "stinking rose." My grandma tended beds of beautiful roses, and even though the aroma of garlic may be quite different from that of roses, I take comfort in being able to draw parallels to her. Like roses, garlic has been grown for centuries; its role in history is significant and connected to nearly all ancient societies.

An Ancient Crop

Garlic is thought to be one of the oldest cultivated crops. Though there is some debate over exact locations, most historians agree the bulbs originated in Central Asia. The earliest bulbs were a form of wild garlic, but the first domesticated crop was grown during Neolithic times in China. From there, the journey of garlic is rich in history, its reach expanding across the globe. Archaeologists discovered clay bulbs in the pyramids of ancient Egypt, as well as papyrus that makes reference to the bulbs 5,000 years ago. Garlic was even used as the local currency during the time of the pharaohs. The spirited vegetable also makes frequent appearances throughout historical texts written by the Babylonians and Chinese. And archaeologists have dated the presence of garlic on the Greek island of Crete back to the years 1850 to 1400 BCE.

As people began to travel and trade around the world, garlic migrated as well. It is thought that Mediterranean nomadic clans frequently used and traded garlic during the Middle Ages. Garlic is believed to have been introduced to Europe, including France, Italy, and Germany, as Crusaders brought bulbs home from the Holy Land for their many healing purposes. The bulbs were grown and spread throughout Europe as countries were conquered, borders were blurred, and families moved. The many superstitious beliefs and the lore surrounding garlic made it a popular choice in medieval gardens, where it was also grown with centuries-old knowledge of its healing properties. Eventually, the flavorful bulbs made their way to North America, packed carefully among the belongings of Polish, Italian, and German immigrants. Garlic became an heirloom vegetable passed down from generation to generation as a way to continue traditions in a new, unfamiliar place.

Garlic is thought to be one of the oldest cultivated crops. . . . The earliest bulbs were a form of wild garlic, but the first domesticated crop was grown during Neolithic times in China.

Garlic in Traditional Medicine

From its earliest days as a cultivated plant, garlic has been grown for its healing properties and healthful attributes. It populated medicinal gardens in ancient China as far back as 2700 BCE, where it was one of the most-used herbal remedies for a broad range of ailments, including insect bites, loss of appetite, and wounds. The healers of ancient India paired garlic tonics with rituals and prayers to combat skin diseases, hemorrhoids, and coughs. The medicinal uses of garlic were even noted in their holy books, the Vedas. In ancient Egypt, impoverished people were known to apply garlic topically to treat skin lesions such as warts or even leprosy.

In some parts of the world, garlic was, and still is, thought to be a powerful aphrodisiac because of its many circulatory benefits—so much so that members of many religious sects, such as Buddhist monks or Catholic nuns, were forbidden to consume garlic. The plague masks of seventeenth-century Europe featured a beaklike nose that doctors would fill with garlic, partially to harness the bulbs' antibacterial properties, as well as to disguise the scent of death. During the years of the Second World War, garlic was called "Russian penicillin" because it was used to treat soldiers as precious antibiotics became scarce. On the steppes of Tibet, garlic has long been grown for a remedy that eases stomachaches. The medicinal uses of garlic continue in current times in the form of home remedies to ward off the common cold and to promote heart health.

Today garlic is a widely popular herbal remedy for many maladies, and there is a huge increase in the number of medical studies being done to test its effectiveness. Natural healers and allopathic doctors alike recognize garlic's many preventive health benefits.

Evolving for Flavor

An estimated 2.5 million acres of garlic are grown worldwide, with the bulb being utilized both in the kitchen and the home medicine cabinet. Even as garlic has been revered for its healing attributes, it has served as a flavor additive for several thousand years. The aromatic bulbs we know today may hail from Central Asia, but they are a prominent ingredient in numerous cultures, each growing a different variety that is acclimated to their region.

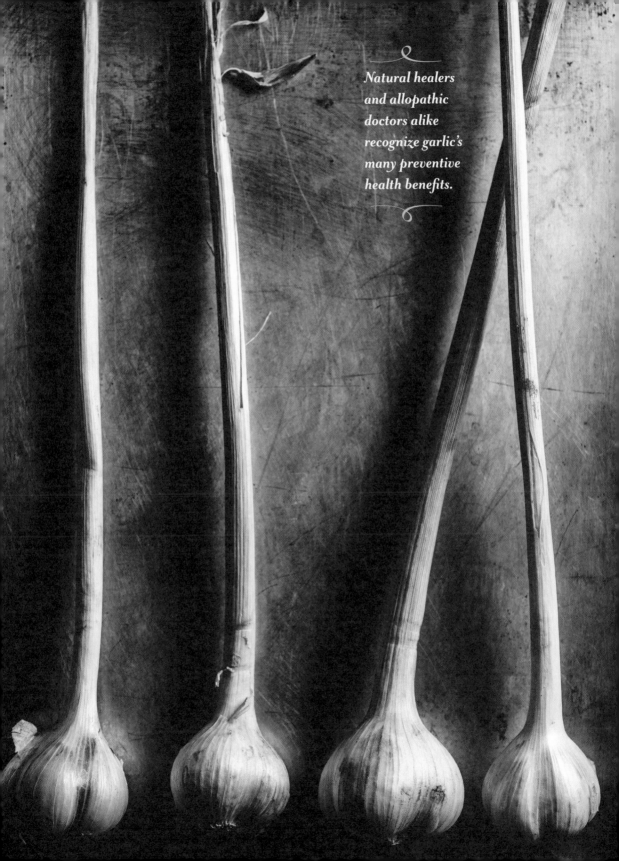

Natural healers and allopathic doctors alike recognize garlic's many preventive health benefits.

Many of the globe's favorite cuisines feature the bold essence of garlic. Each region's food tradition, however, offers a unique expression of garlic's flavor by pairing it with distinctive local herbs and spices. For example, Mediterranean cuisines use robust herbs such as basil, thyme, rosemary, oregano, and parsley alongside garlic to season their dishes, whereas in Korea, garlic is combined with the spiciness of fresh ginger. That is what makes cooking with garlic so interesting: You can create meals from around the world with just one bulb. Garlic is considered a universal ingredient, served in more diverse cuisines than almost any other food.

Garlic in Folklore

The fragrant globes play an important role in the history and folklore of quite a few world cultures. For some, garlic bulbs hold significance in dreams: It is thought to be extremely lucky to dream of garlic in the house, and dreaming of eating garlic is said to predict that the dreamer will soon discover hidden secrets. Using garlic to ward off evil is also a common theme. The bulbs are viewed as a powerful talisman, protecting all who surround themselves with the pungent fragrance.

In Egypt, well-preserved bulbs were found in centuries-old tombs of pharaohs, placed there to protect their leaders in the afterlife. There are reports of Greek midwives hanging heads of garlic in birthing rooms to deter evil spirits and serve as an offering to Hecate, the goddess of childbirth, for a safe delivery. Some historians say that long ago it was even common practice for central Europeans to wear necklaces made of the cloves or to rub fresh garlic on their chimneys to expel demons. The beautiful braids of garlic that we know and love today are thought to originate from this very purpose: to hang above kitchen windows for the safekeeping of the home's owners. Brides in ancient Roman times carried bouquets of strong-smelling garlic and herbs instead of flowers to protect the couple against evil spirits that might disrupt the wedding.

Not all garlic lore is concerned with combating evil. Some societies associated the overpowering fragrance of the bulbs with strength and force. Athletes in ancient Greece would consume garlic cloves before competitions to ensure enhanced power, strength, and endurance. Similarly, Roman generals would often plant fields of garlic in the countries that they conquered because the bulb was believed to provide their armies with courage.

The Spice and Social Class

While today garlic and the dishes it flavors are known for bringing people together, historically garlic divided people in some cultures. In ancient Egypt, Egyptian royals gave enslaved people and workers garlic to keep them strong, so the pyramids could be constructed more quickly.

In Europe during the Middle Ages, spices were extremely rare and expensive; garlic, in contrast, grew plentiful and was a cheap ingredient. Italian nobles demonstrated their higher social status by cooking with rare, highly sought-after ingredients, whereas the working class routinely ate dishes flavored with garlic. The unmistakable stench of garlic on the breath was considered a sign of the lower class. Peasants were often derogatorily referred to as "garlic eaters," while aristocrats avoided the pungent flavor at all costs. In fact, Alfonso XI of Spain, King of Castile and León in the eleventh century, was rumored to have punished members of his court who smelled of garlic.

LEFT: Workers and enslaved people who built the pyramids were given garlic to keep their strength up.

BOTTOM RIGHT: According to Romanian folklore, garlic kept away evil spirits; strings of garlic were hung over doorways for protection. Shown is a Romanian garlic seller.

As time went on, the full-bodied aroma of garlic become more alluring. Ennobling garlic began as sixteenth-century Italian chefs paired garlic with more exclusive ingredients, such as expensive meats and cheeses, in order to elevate garlic's standing. Eventually, the bulb became more accepted in aristocratic society and grew in popularity throughout many cuisines around the world.

Garlic and Vampires

And, of course, there are the tales of vampires. Most of us have heard the stories of fanged beings with long black capes who are repelled by the pungent cloves. Vampire lore hails mostly from Transylvania (present-day Romania), coincidentally the same region where a softneck variety, 'Transylvanian Garlic', most likely originated. It's no wonder that the bulbs make frequent appearances in rituals to ward off Dracula and his minions.

FOOD FRIGHTS

It never fails: Someone will stop by my market table with a goofy grin and say, "Bet you don't have any vampires on your farm!" Halloween has always been one of my favorite holidays, so I've enjoyed creating a line of vampire-themed products. In October our Garlic Scape Powder transforms into "Zombie Dust," and fresh bulbs of garlic are sold as "Vampire Repellent." It's all in good fun, putting a spooky spin on our garlic for a few weeks! The vampire connections come naturally to most people, so why not run with it?

Believe it or not, there is some truth to it all. Maybe not to the actual presence of vampires themselves, but to garlic's working against sinister forces, because during medieval European times, sickness was often seen as a scourge or work of evil. Priests would be called in before a healer in hopes of repelling wicked forces. Garlic is a natural immune booster, and while the scientific mechanisms may not have been known at the time, healers did recognize that garlic could, in fact, aid in treating illnesses. Rest assured that your home and loved ones will be well protected once you start harvesting your garlic bulbs.

Garlic for Health

The list of garlic's health benefits is quite long. Many research studies suggest that people who ingest garlic regularly are less likely to catch a cold, and the cloves are commonly used as an herbal supplement to help maintain a healthy immune system. Garlic is also widely touted as a supplement for heart health because of its anti-inflammatory effects: The cloves offer high amounts of vitamins that can help lower blood pressure and cholesterol levels. Studies have even shown that garlic is helpful in fighting foodborne illness because its diallyl sulfide is thought to be 100 times more effective than two popular antibiotics. The health benefits from garlic can be obtained by adding it (in moderation) to your diet, or even taking it in the form of garlic pills. Use caution when eating raw garlic, since the cloves in their natural state have a fiery bite and can cause severe heartburn.

The healthful constituents of garlic include:

- Vitamins C and B6, both of which play a role in maintaining a healthy immune system.

- Manganese, which helps enzymes within the body break down carbohydrates, proteins, and cholesterol.

- Allicin, a powerful antioxidant that can help our bodies block free radicals. Free radicals can harm and alter the makeup of other cells and have been implicated in heart disease.

- Zinc, which aids in the healthy growth of cells within the body.

A World of Garlic Varieties

There are two main types of garlic: hardneck and softneck. The term *neck* refers to the stalk portion of the plant. Hardneck garlic varieties have a noticeable rigid central stalk (which forms a scape—a long, leafless flower stalk), whereas softneck garlic grows a soft and pliable stem (and no scape). Each type has many different varieties known for their distinct traits in both growing and cooking.

Hardneck

Hardneck varieties tend to be the hardiest—and thus are better for growing in a northern climate. The bulbs are quite cold-tolerant and thrive in cool growing zones (USDA Hardiness Zone 5 and below). Their plants can often withstand sporadic light spring frosts (low temperatures of 32°F/0°C). Hardneck garlic varieties are vigorous producers and offer the additional harvest of garlic scapes, an early-summer treat. Their bold flavors make them highly sought after. However, their storage life is slightly shorter than softneck varieties.

There are well over 200 different varieties of hardneck garlic, in eight main categories:

- Porcelain
- Rocambole
- Purple stripe
- Glazed purple stripe
- Marbled purple stripe
- Asiatic
- Turba
- Creole

ALL ABOUT ALLICIN

Allicin plays a key role in the characteristic boldness of garlic. The sulfur compound is what gives garlic its heat as well as its many healthful powers, such as the ability to fight infections, lower cholesterol, and protect the body from free radicals. Cutting, chopping, or chewing garlic activates the alliinase enzyme found within the fresh cloves, which then converts the sulfoxide alliin into allicin. Interestingly enough, the production of allicin is a defense mechanism of garlic plants, designed to protect them from pests.

Heating garlic can diminish the effect of allicin, but there is what is known as the "10-minute rule" to counterbalance this: Let crushed garlic sit for 10 minutes before cooking to maximize its health benefits. The resting time allows the allicin levels to reach their full potential and prevents loss of allicin during the cooking process.

SOFTNECK

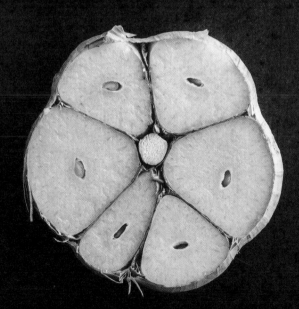

HARDNECK

Hardneck
Here are a few varieties I have grown on my farm.

'MUSIC'
'Music' is known for producing jumbo bulbs and remarkably large cloves, making it ideal as a roasting bulb. It is extremely cold-tolerant, an excellent choice for northern gardens.

- **Category:** porcelain hardneck
- **Average number of cloves:** 4 to 5; fewer but larger cloves
- **Storage length:** 4 to 6 months
- **Flavor notes:** smooth and robust

'GEORGIAN FIRE'
The name says it all about these beautiful white bulbs—this variety is hot!

- **Category:** porcelain hardneck
- **Average number of cloves:** 5 to 7
- **Storage length:** 5 to 7 months
- **Flavor notes:** aggressively spicy

'YUGOSLAVIAN'
Originates from Eastern Europe and is a reliable grower in cold climates.

- **Category:** porcelain hardneck
- **Average number of cloves:** 5 to 7
- **Storage length:** 4 to 6 months
- **Flavor notes:** spicy

'RED RUSSIAN'
Known for its striking purple wrappers and intense flavor, 'Red Russian' is very hardy and produces dependable yields of large bulbs.

- **Category:** marbled purple stripe hardneck
- **Average number of cloves:** 4 to 6
- **Storage length:** 5 to 7 months
- **Flavor notes:** spicy and bold

'PURPLE RUSSIAN'
'Purple Russian' is closely related to 'Red Russian', but with a slightly milder garlicky flavor, making it a favored culinary variety.

- **Category:** marbled purple stripe hardneck
- **Average number of cloves:** 4 to 6
- **Storage length:** 5 to 7 months
- **Flavor notes:** very pleasant, smooth

'MUSIC'

'RED RUSSIAN'

'GEORGIAN
FIRE'

'YUGOSLAVIAN'

'PURPLE
RUSSIAN'

'TIBETAN'

'SPANISH
ROJA'

'PERSIAN
STAR'

'GERMAN
RED'

'CHESNOK
RED'

Hardneck

'TIBETAN'

Extraordinary purple striped bulbs that produce beautiful pink cloves. 'Tibetan' tends to be the first variety to pop up in spring.

- **Category:** purple stripe hardneck
- **Average number of cloves:** 8 to 12 (higher number of smaller cloves)
- **Storage length:** 6 to 8 months
- **Flavor notes:** bold, aromatic

'PERSIAN STAR'

A well-known heirloom variety that produces umbels (flower clusters) with a high number of bulbils (tiny secondary bulbs).

- **Category:** purple stripe hardneck
- **Average number of cloves:** 8 to 12
- **Storage length:** 6 to 8 months
- **Flavor notes:** rich, not too overpowering

'CHESNOK RED'

Known for its medicinal properties, 'Chesnok Red' has a long history of being used in herbal medicine because of its very high levels of allicin.

- **Category:** purple stripe hardneck
- **Average number of cloves:** 8 to 10
- **Storage length:** 6 to 8 months
- **Flavor notes:** mild and pleasing, slightly sweet

'SPANISH ROJA'

These bulbs can be a little trickier to grow because of their thin and somewhat loose wrappers. They require an extra-gentle touch when it comes time to harvest, but they are well worth the effort.

- **Category:** rocambole
- **Average number of cloves:** 6 to 10
- **Storage length:** 4 to 6 months
- **Flavor notes:** full-bodied with beautiful aroma

'GERMAN RED'

A garlic that is a treat for your taste buds and nose, 'German Red' is a consistent large bulb producer.

- **Category:** rocambole
- **Average number of cloves:** 5 to 6
- **Storage length:** 4 to 6 months
- **Flavor notes:** medium heat

Softneck

Softneck garlic bulbs are composed of many layered cloves. If you've ever bought garlic from a grocery store, chances are it was a softneck variety. They are known for their long storage ability, often lasting up to a year from harvest, and their characteristic pliable stems make them the ideal garlic for traditional braiding. These bulbs grow best in warm climates with mild winters (USDA Hardiness Zone 6 and above) and are generally not suitable for regions with harsh winters. That said, I still encourage you fellow northern gardeners to try. Gardening is often done mostly by trial and error, and sometimes attempting something new can be incredibly rewarding.

There are two main categories of softneck garlic: artichoke and silverskin. Artichoke bulbs are larger and have a milder flavor than the bulbs of silverskin varieties.

'CALIFORNIA WHITE'
A classic garlic variety that has had some success being grown in cooler zones.

- **Category:** artichoke
- **Average number of cloves:** 10 to 16
- **Storage length:** 9 to 12 months
- **Flavor notes:** mild but pleasing

'SILVER ROSE'
An excellent variety for creating traditional garlic braids because of their extended shelf life (making the braids last longer) as well as their soft, pliable necks; commonly grown in Italy and France.

- **Category:** silverskin
- **Average number of cloves:** 10 to 12
- **Storage length:** 12 months
- **Flavor notes:** well rounded

ELEPHANT GARLIC

Elephant garlic (*Allium ampeloprasum*) is not actually a true garlic. Though there are many similarities between the two species, elephant garlic is closer in origin to leeks than to garlic and tastes more like a leek as well. Its misleading name came from the presence of a bulb and cloves that resemble garlic.

Elephant garlic is a biennial vegetable, meaning it requires two full life cycles (seasons) to produce a mature bulb. It grows best in warm, humid climates (USDA Hardiness Zones 6–9). Elephant garlic is planted in a similar fashion to true garlic, with each clove being used as a seed. During the first year, elephant garlic plants will produce only a large single clove; it isn't until the second season that proper cloves for replanting will develop. Much like garlic, the bulbs require a drying time after harvest and can be stored to be enjoyed throughout winter.

Elephant garlic can be harvested in either the first or second year. The gigantic bulbs are a widely popular choice for roasting and serving whole. Since their flavor is much milder than that of their garlic cousins, most garlic lovers would argue that even though elephant garlic is quite delicious in its own way, it does not make a suitable substitute for real garlic.

'CALIFORNIA WHITE'

'SILVER ROSE'

ELEPHANT GARLIC

Explore Garlic in Your Community

Whether you are looking for more information on the history of garlic, fresh ingredients to cook with, or growing tips, it's easy to connect with your community over a shared love of garlic! Farmers' markets and festivals are excellent places to start. You can also explore local farms and garlic growers in your area by joining a garlic club. Through common goals and a sense of kinship, garlic lovers excitedly come together to celebrate an abundance of their favorite crop.

Farmers' Markets

Frequent your local farmers' markets in summer or fall for fresh garlic options. Shopping locally allows you to connect with the people who actually grow your food, giving you the chance to learn about their growing practices. There are many nutritional benefits to eating locally harvested produce, since vital nutrients are lost in lengthy transportation times.

Markets feature a friendly and inclusive atmosphere. With farmers coming together from near and far, you will more than likely find multiple new varieties of garlic to sample. Take the opportunity to taste the differences in each type of garlic and ask for new ideas for using them.

Garlic Festivals

Garlic festivals are held throughout much of the world, so chances are you won't have to travel far to find one. Most of these events take place at the end of the growing season, in fall after the harvest is completed and the bulbs have finished drying. Festivalgoers can expect to be treated to the smell of roasting garlic wafting through the air as they shop at merchant booths selling garlic-themed wares. Friendly competitions ensue in the form of garlic-peeling races or the highly coveted prize for the best homegrown bulbs. Best of all, everybody who attends undoubtedly shares an overpowering love of garlic!

One of the more memorable aspects of garlic festivals is, of course, the food. There are often garlic tasting bars that offer up slices of raw garlic so the consumer can pick out subtle tasting notes of different varieties. Cooks push the boundaries of culinary garlic in collaborative cook-offs and featured dishes for festivalgoers to enjoy. Unique garlic treats are in no short supply. They even make garlic ice cream, a daring and extremely creamy delicacy. (See page 61 for my sorbet recipe.) The flavor profiles range from subtle to aggressively strong but are sure to win over the taste buds of everyone from the garlic curious to the garlic fanatic.

GARLIC FESTIVAL

TRADE ENTRANCE →

GILROY

FRASSETTI BROS

MY HIRASAKI

B & T FARMS

CAPITAL

Garlic-centered events are also a place for growers to share their love for the flavorful bulbs. These gatherings encourage direct competitors to choose companionship above all else. The fun and energetic environment creates an opportunity to bask in the success of another harvest and to commiserate in the sorrow of seasonal obstacles and hardships.

Sourcing Varieties to Grow

A local farmers' market or festival is a great place to search for seed garlic so that you can grow your own. Find a garlic grower close to home to supply you with bulbs that are best suited to your hardiness zone. Look for big bulbs to yield strong future crops, and perhaps discover a new variety to try as well; festivals, in particular, are a great place to find a range of varieties. You may just become a garlic collector!

When it comes to cooking with homegrown garlic, a little goes a long way; fresh garlic is more potent than store-bought. Another added benefit of homegrown garlic is the sheer size of the cloves. Depending on the variety you choose to grow, an individual clove may reach 2 inches in size! For example, one clove of 'Music' can often equal three or four store-bought cloves.

JOIN A GARLIC CLUB OR CSA

Joining a Garlic of the Month Club or a garlic CSA (community-supported agriculture) program is a great way to surround yourself with like-minded individuals. Essentially, a CSA membership buys a share of the bounty, be that garden vegetables, meat cuts, or garlic. The member accepts the risks of growing at the mercy of the elements alongside the many rewards of eating naturally grown local produce. The farmer in turn has the support of their community before the season starts, so they can plan accordingly. It creates a beautiful relationship between farmer and consumer.

Many farms host CSA programs that are catered to what they have to offer. By signing up for a garlic CSA or club, you are joining a community of garlic lovers who rejoice in the seasonal ingredients available. You can almost always expect to receive garlic scapes during the summer program, while the later months of the year will most likely include different types of garlic bulbs to cook with. Your membership will give you a chance to try new products (such as salts or dip mixes) and help producers glean valuable insight on how to improve their offerings. Better yet, garlic farms often organize tours for club members!

My garlic CSA program is made up of three carefully curated boxes of garlicky treats. I try to include something different in each one, as well as a new recipe for members to try. The most unique offering was a box of black garlic macarons made by a local baker. The cookies featured a dark chocolate fudge center with a small piece of black garlic. The CSA members loved them.

Garlic tends to be one of those ingredients that people measure with their hearts.

2

COOK AND EAT

recipes celebrating garlicky goodness

Widely used and versatile, garlic exhibits
many different layers of flavor. On one
side, there is the bold, often overpoweringly
sharp taste of raw cloves; on the other
side is the sweet, almost caramel-like flavor
of preserved black garlic. In the middle,
flavorwise, are roasted garlic bulbs—smooth
as velvet when they hit your palate, they
exhibit a delicate balance of spicy and
sweet that's created as heat tones down
pungency and brings out sugars.

Inspired by Family and the Love of Garlic

The alluring notes of flavorful garlic-focused dishes are guaranteed to draw family and friends to your table to celebrate life's riches, including good, wholesome food. Garlic, favored by so many, is an inviting, comforting flavor. Whether you're hosting an elaborate garden party or cooking a simple meal for your family, the collection of recipes in this chapter will help you use fresh, local ingredients.

Most of these recipes have been inspired by the lifetime I've spent watching and working in the kitchens of the extraordinary women in my family. With an unparalleled ability to make everyone feel special, my mom always has a place set at the table for "strays," or unexpected guests; she has shown me that the art of cooking goes far beyond the simple ingredients. I was raised with a deep understanding that food is love and that to provide culinary enjoyment for others is to nourish them.

Of course, recipes are more like guidelines for true garlic lovers, who add garlic to their heart's content, not according to the suggested amount in the recipe!

Cooking with Garlic through the Seasons

Even though garlic can be best categorized as a winter storage crop, there are endless ways to enjoy the flavorful bulbs throughout the year. Each season offers a unique form of garlic, ensuring that your taste buds will never be bored. In fall, the taste of the first fresh bulbs is eagerly anticipated. The winter months leave you craving warm comfort foods rich in flavor, as you make your way through your stored bulbs. Springtime can often be seen as a lean garlic period; however, with a little extra work, you can appreciate the boldness of freshly ground garlic powder. Garlic scapes are an embodiment of the taste of summer, their short season meant to be enjoyed to the fullest extent. Eating seasonally gives you a chance to further explore the many uses of your garlic crop in the kitchen.

Add garlic to your heart's content—not the suggested amount in the recipe!

Fall

At this point of the year, fresh garlic is readily available and revered for its incredible flavors. Farmers' markets and festivals celebrate the return of a favored harvest, and there's palpable excitement as customers seek specific varieties. As the days get shorter and nighttime temperatures dip a little lower, I am often drawn to comfort foods and festive aromas coming from the oven. There are few things I love more than the intoxicating smell of freshly roasted garlic! Whether you are enjoying the spoils of your first crop or sourcing an ingredient locally, I think that you, too, will realize that a moody fall day is the best time to create a garlic-forward dish.

FAVORITE GARLIC RECIPES FOR FALL
Barbecued Roasted Garlic (page 55), Roasted Garlic and
Sage Butter (page 58), Black Garlic and Caramel Mini Cheesecakes
(page 103), Roasted Carrots with Black Garlic Glaze (page 96)

Winter

Even though garlic in the fields sleeps through winter, the season is full of life in the kitchen. Due to their rather short growing window, most northern zones are privy to only one garlic harvest annually, resulting in a large gap in fresh bulb sources during the late winter and spring months. Fresh, stored bulbs are still available in early winter, but by midwinter when our supply is running low, we use more preserved garlic. By processing our garlic, we can offer flavorful alternatives throughout that period—or at least until garlic scape season starts! When it comes to preserving garlic, I like dehydrating or freezing methods best (see page 212). There are also delicious recipes for slow-roasted bulbs, garlic powders, and even savory butters.

Winter is the time to embrace rich foods that warm you from the inside out. Eating seasonally, as well as locally, can be challenging and often requires extra prep time to ensure you get the most out of your ingredients, but the rewards are immeasurable. Not only do you support your local economy but you also reap the benefits of vital nutrients in products that are fresh or were preserved when fresh. The trick is to allow yourself to be creative and luxuriate in the farm-to-table (or garden-to-table) experience.

FAVORITE GARLIC RECIPES FOR WINTER
Garlic Confit (page 43), Immune Booster Soup (page 48),
Honey Garlic Ribs (page 51), Savory Shortbread Cookies (page 113)

Spring

You will likely notice a shift in the kitchen as bulbs—fresh or preserved—become scarce. This is a great time to turn to stores of granulated garlic (finely ground dehydrated garlic cloves or scapes) to achieve the optimal flavor in most dishes. Making your own garlic powders locks in the powerful-tasting notes of homegrown garlic. A little goes a long way!

There is also the exciting addition of green garlic, which is the young, immature garlic plant. At this stage of the plant's life, the notoriously strong roots have not fully developed and can be pulled easily from the soil. Just keep in mind that each green garlic pulled from your garden is one fewer bulb for fall or winter.

Green garlic brings taste buds back to life, awakening them after a long winter. The entire plant is edible at this point and can be cooked similarly to scallions. They are a flavorful addition to spring salads. The white immature bulb can be chopped and sautéed, useful for creating enticing soups or omelets.

FAVORITE GARLIC RECIPES FOR SPRING
Grandma's Garlic Cabbage Slaw (page 114), Black Garlic–Chocolate Chip Cookies (page 100), Garlic Scape Croutons (page 118), Black Garlic Mac and Cheese (page 98)

Summer

The summer season is bursting with garlic! From garlic scapes in July to fresh bulbs in August, the pungent, herbaceous flavor of garlic is never lacking.

Garlic scapes are the first of the summer garlic and can be used in place of the cloves until the fresh bulbs become available. One of the best ways to prepare garlic scapes is to grill them with a light brushing of oil in a cast-iron pan, but there are endless possibilities to help you become better acquainted with this unique ingredient.

Although the fresh bulbs require drying time before storage, they can be used in the kitchen right away. Long harvest days are often rewarded with roasted garlic, fresh off the barbecue. Allow yourself the pleasure of enjoying the bounty of the season—just remember to save enough for winter!

FAVORITE GARLIC RECIPES FOR SUMMER
Garlic Scape Pesto (page 67), Fresh Garlic Scape Salsa (page 81),
Roasted Garlic and Nasturtium Cheeseball (page 57)

recipes *for* fresh garlic

These garlic-forward recipes will leave you with a renewed appreciation for the pungent cloves. Whether used as a standout ingredient or added in a more subtle fashion to enhance other seasonings, garlic entices the senses. Follow your taste buds to find unique and exciting recipes that highlight the use of garlic in the kitchen. Enjoy all the flavors and the many different ways to experience them.

Garlic Confit

Garlic confit utilizes a French method of slowly cooking foods in fat until they are tender. The cloves are simmered at a low heat in oil, so that their flavor mellows and becomes decadently rich.

YIELD: 2 CUPS

- 10 medium-sized garlic bulbs (about 2 cups cloves)
- 2 bay leaves
- 2 fresh rosemary sprigs
- ¼ teaspoon red pepper flakes
- 1 cup olive oil

1 Preheat the oven to 300°F (150°C).

2 Crack the garlic bulbs apart and peel the individual cloves.

3 Place the cloves in a small ovenproof baking dish. Add the bay leaves, rosemary, and pepper flakes. Cover with the oil.

4 Bake for 90 minutes. Store the cloves and oil, covered, in the refrigerator for up to 1 week.

Garlic Confit Flatbread Pizza

For many years my partner, Paul, and I treated ourselves to a similar pizza while in Vancouver, British Columbia. We were inspired to try to make an at-home version and really enjoy adding foraged Saskatoon berries to it. Saskatoon berries grow wild throughout the Canadian Prairies and many parts of the northern United States. They look like a blueberry but have a sweet flavor that is quite unique. You can substitute blackberries if Saskatoon berries are not available.

YIELD: 2-3 SERVINGS

1 tablespoon extra-virgin olive oil

1 (10-inch) flatbread (homemade or store-bought)

6 slices prosciutto

¼ cup cloves from Garlic Confit (page 43)

¼ cup Saskatoon berries

½ cup arugula

¼ cup shaved parmesan cheese

1 Preheat the oven to 400°F (200°C).

2 Spread the oil on the flatbread.

3 Layer the prosciutto over the flatbread. Arrange the garlic and berries evenly on top. Add the arugula and sprinkle on the parmesan.

4 Bake for 12 to 15 minutes, until the cheese has melted and browned.

PEELING GARLIC CLOVES

Peeling the cloves is everyone's least favorite part of cooking with garlic.
Here are a few tricks to make the task easier.

• Use a silicone garlic peeler. They are incredibly easy to use. Just roll the cloves
back and forth within the tunnel a few times to remove the hulls.

• Soak the cloves in cold water for 30 minutes prior to peeling. The papery husks
soften in the water, making them easy to remove.

• Place the garlic cloves in a stainless steel bowl. Place a second stainless bowl
upside down on top of the first. Grasp the bowls firmly together and shake the
cloves to release the hulls.

Herbed Garlic Bread

Being able to cook with fresh herbs is one of the best parts of growing a garden. The herbs add so much depth to the flavor of this buttery garlic bread that every piece will be quickly devoured.

YIELD: 8 SERVINGS

½ cup (1 stick) butter, softened

2 garlic cloves, minced

1 teaspoon finely chopped fresh dill

¼ teaspoon freshly ground black pepper

1 teaspoon finely chopped fresh parsley

1 loaf French bread or baguette

1 cup shredded mozzarella cheese (optional)

1 Preheat the oven to 375°F (190°C).

2 Mix together the butter, garlic, dill, pepper, and half of the parsley in a small bowl.

3 Cut the bread loaf in half lengthwise. Generously spread the butter mixture onto each half. Sprinkle the cheese, if using, over the butter. Top with the remaining parsley.

4 Place the loaf on a baking sheet and bake, uncovered, for 12 to 15 minutes, until golden, or the cheese, if using, is bubbly.

Immune Booster Soup

At the first sign of a cold, I whip up a pot of this soup. Its warmth is so comforting, and the powerful health benefits of garlic can be savored in every spoonful. It is chock-full of good ingredients and provides a great immune boost for the winter months.

YIELD: 4 SERVINGS

1 teaspoon butter

1 medium-sized carrot, peeled and cut into small pieces

2 stalks celery, cut into small pieces

10–12 garlic cloves, minced

4 cups chicken broth

2 bay leaves

1 teaspoon fresh thyme

4 medium-sized potatoes, peeled and cubed

Salt and freshly ground black pepper

1 Melt the butter in a large soup pot over medium-high heat. Add the carrot and celery and cook until tender, 8 to 10 minutes. Add the garlic and cook until aromatic, 3 to 4 minutes.

2 Scrape to loosen any flavorful bits stuck to the bottom of the pot. Add the broth, bay leaves, and thyme. Bring to a boil, then reduce the heat and let simmer for about 10 minutes.

3 Add the potatoes and cook until tender, about 20 minutes. Remove and discard the bay leaves, and season the soup to taste with salt and pepper.

4 Enjoy immediately, or refrigerate for up to 3 days.

DON'T OVERCOOK

The flavor of overcooked or burnt garlic is extremely bitter, so it is important to cook garlic carefully. Keep a close eye on it while it cooks in the pan, stirring often to avoid any browning.

Honey Garlic Ribs

This recipe has been a favorite of mine ever since I was a little girl, when my mom would let my sister and me choose a special meal for our birthdays each year. Mine was always Honey Garlic Ribs! These are messy and so flavorful—the perfect combination for saucy ribs.

YIELD: 4 SERVINGS

¼ cup packed brown sugar

1½ tablespoons cornstarch

½ teaspoon dry mustard

½ cup ketchup

½ cup honey

¼ cup apple cider vinegar

¼ cup soy sauce

4 garlic cloves, finely minced

1 rack of pork ribs

1 Preheat the oven to 350°F (180°C).

2 Combine the sugar, cornstarch, and mustard in a small mixing bowl. Add the ketchup, honey, vinegar, soy sauce, and garlic. Stir until well combined.

3 Cut the ribs apart, spread them on a rimmed baking sheet, and coat with approximately half of the marinade.

4 Bake for 45 minutes, then turn ribs and baste with the remaining marinade. Bake for 45 minutes longer, until the sauce thickens.

Garlic Ginger Beef

The bold seasonings in this dish only get better as time goes on, making the leftovers something you will truly look forward to. Serve over rice or rice noodles with steamed broccoli, carrots, and scallions, and garnish with sesame seeds.

YIELD: 4 SERVINGS

1	pound lean ground beef
½	cup honey
¼	cup soy sauce
2	tablespoons sesame oil
1	tablespoon red pepper flakes
1	teaspoon peeled and grated fresh ginger
3–4	garlic cloves, minced
	Sesame seeds, for garnish

1 Brown the ground beef in a large skillet over medium heat.

2 Meanwhile, combine the honey, soy sauce, oil, pepper flakes, ginger, and garlic in a medium bowl. Mix well.

3 Pour the honey mixture over the beef and simmer over low heat until the sauce thickens slightly, 3 to 5 minutes.

4 Garnish with sesame seeds.

recipes *for* roasted garlic

Roasting garlic transforms its familiar spiciness to a softer, more delicate flavor. The cooking process results in a dramatically different character, giving garlic a wider range of use. Taste the surprisingly dreamy combination of roasted garlic and honey in a homemade sorbet, or experience the unforgettable addition of a roasted garlic bulb to your charcuterie spread. No matter how you decide to use it, you will truly savor the rich, almost buttery texture of a whole roasted bulb.

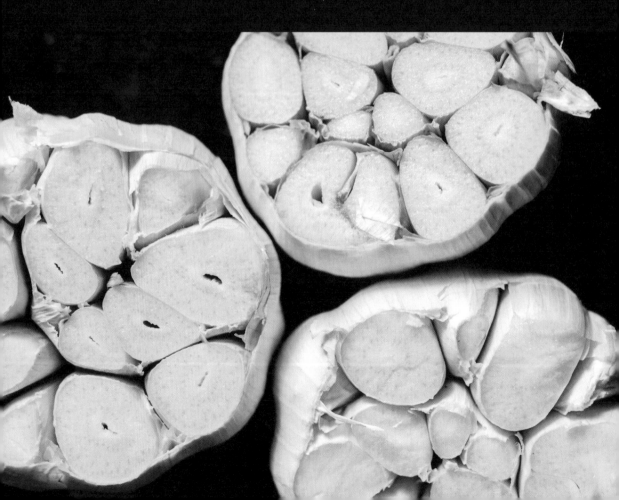

Barbecued Roasted Garlic

Roasting garlic is an easy method to achieve a deep, mellow flavor. This creamy and slightly caramelized garlic is not only beautiful when served as a whole bulb but also adds a smooth finish to any garlic dish. Although garlic can be roasted in the oven, using a grill adds a hint of smoke for an alluring flavor. This garlic is delicious spread on fresh bread.

YIELD: 1 BULB

1 garlic bulb

1 tablespoon olive oil

Pinch of salt

1 Preheat a grill to 400°F (200°C).

2 Cut off the very top of the garlic bulb, so just the tips of the cloves are exposed. Place it on a piece of heavy-duty foil. Drizzle the bulb with the oil and sprinkle it with the salt. Wrap the foil tightly around the bulb.

3 Roast the bulb on the top rack of the grill for approximately 30 minutes, until the cloves are soft when you squeeze the bulb.

4 Scoop out the cloves with a butter knife, or squeeze the bulb to remove the cloves from their skin.

Roasted Garlic and Nasturtium Cheeseball

Edible flowers serve a dual purpose in the garden: to attract pollinators and to be enjoyed in fancy meals. There are many different types (violas, bachelor buttons, begonias), but nasturtiums are one of my favorites because of their peppery flavor. Serve this cheeseball with your favorite crackers or fresh bread.

YIELD: 12 SERVINGS

¼ cup (8–10) nasturtiums or other edible flowers

1 (8-ounce) block cream cheese, softened

½ cup shredded mozzarella cheese

1 teaspoon finely chopped fresh oregano

1 teaspoon finely chopped fresh rosemary

1 teaspoon finely chopped fresh thyme

1 roasted garlic bulb (see page 55)

1 Pluck the petals from the nasturtiums and tear them into small pieces. Set aside.

2 Combine the cream cheese, mozzarella, oregano, rosemary, and thyme in a medium bowl.

3 Squeeze the roasted garlic bulb to remove the cloves from their skin. Add the cloves to the cream cheese mixture and stir until well combined. Gently fold in the flower petals.

4 Shape the cheese mixture into a ball. Wrap it in plastic or beeswax wrap and refrigerate for at least 1 hour before serving.

Roasted Garlic *and* Sage Butter

The recipe calls for both roasted garlic and fresh cloves for a dramatic, full-bodied flavor. The combination of roasted garlic and sage reminds me of autumn harvests. This makes a great finishing butter for steaks.

YIELD: ½ CUP OR 4 SERVINGS

1 roasted garlic bulb (see page 55)

2 garlic cloves, minced

½ cup unsalted butter, softened

1 tablespoon minced fresh sage

1 Squeeze the roasted garlic bulb to remove the cloves from their skin.

2 Combine the roasted cloves, minced cloves, butter, and sage in a medium mixing bowl. Use an electric mixer to whip the mixture until well combined.

3 Scrape the butter mixture onto a sheet of parchment paper and form it into a log.

4 Let stand for at least 30 minutes before serving to allow the flavors to meld.

NATURAL HONEY

A few years ago, I dove headfirst into the fascinating and intricate world of honeybees with two small hives located just outside my garden. Honeybee society has lasted millennia, and each bee has a specific role to play. The foragers leave the safety of the hive in search of sweet, precious nectar, often flying up to five miles from their home. Each type of flower they visit provides a different color and flavor of pollen. Sunflowers, for example, hold pollen that is a deep golden tone, whereas pollen from poppies is nearly black. The varying nectars contribute to a wide range of subtle differences in honey flavors. My province is home to vast fields of canola that, with the help of the honeybees, produce a very fragrant white honey. My personal favorite is a clover honey that is extremely floral in taste. Natural honey is one of life's little luxuries, best harvested and enjoyed in small amounts so there is always more than enough left for the bees.

Roasted Garlic *and* Honey Sorbet

No garlic celebration is complete without a roasted garlic sorbet! This no-churn, dairy-free version features sweet, caramelized notes of roasted garlic alongside fragrant floral honey. The lemon adds a slight zest that lingers on the palate.

YIELD: 6-8 SERVINGS

> 1 cup water
>
> 1 cup sugar
>
> 1 roasted garlic bulb (see page 55)
>
> ¼ cup creamed honey
>
> 2 tablespoons lemon juice

1 Combine the water and sugar in a medium saucepan. Stir until the sugar dissolves. Bring to a boil, then remove from the heat. Let cool completely.

2 Squeeze the roasted garlic bulb to remove the cloves from their skin. Transfer to a medium mixing bowl and add the honey. Use an electric mixer to cream the garlic and honey together.

3 Transfer the cooled sugar water to a blender. Add the garlic-honey mixture and the lemon juice. Blend until smooth.

4 Transfer the mixture to a metal loaf pan. Freeze, uncovered, for at least 6 hours before serving. Store leftovers in an airtight freezer-safe container for up to 6 months.

garlic scape recipes

You will fall in love with garlic scapes once you start cooking with them! The wacky curls create eye-catching displays on plates while adding a garlicky kick to pestos, pastas, and aromatic garlic butters. Garlic scapes have a snappy texture and are tender when harvested young. Their mellow garlic flavor tastes of summer—they are truly a fun ingredient to play with.

Garlic scapes keep extremely well, often lasting for weeks if stored properly. Find tips on how best to store them on page 199.

Grilled Garlic Scapes

I don't know about you, but I think everything tastes better with the smoky char that comes from grilling on a barbecue. Garlic scapes are no exception—the grilled curlicues make an excellent side dish. You can choose to place the scapes directly on the grill, but I find using a cast-iron pan or grill basket keeps them from falling between the grates.

YIELD: 4–6 SERVINGS

15–20 garlic scapes

1 tablespoon vegetable oil

½ teaspoon salt

¼ teaspoon paprika

¼ teaspoon freshly ground black pepper

1 Preheat a grill to 400 to 425°F (200 to 220°C).

2 Prepare the scapes by trimming any woody or hard parts off the stalk. Place in a large bowl and toss with the oil. Season with the salt, paprika, and pepper. Toss to evenly coat.

3 Place the garlic scapes in a cast-iron pan. Set on the grill and cook until tender and slightly charred, 8 to 10 minutes.

Mint *and* Garlic Scape Butter

This refreshing and savory butter freezes well, so you can enjoy its summery flavor all year long.

YIELD: 1 POUND OR 8 SERVINGS

1 pound butter, softened

¾ cup finely minced garlic scapes

¼ cup finely chopped mint

1 Combine the butter and garlic scapes in the bowl of a stand mixer. Mix until smooth, then fold in the mint.

2 Turn out the butter mixture onto a piece of waxed paper. Roll into a log.

3 Cut into ½-inch slices. Use right away or freeze for up to 6 months.

HARVESTING WILD MINT

Wild mint, a bold cousin to cultivated varieties, grows abundantly along our farm's riverbanks. It flourishes in damp areas and has been foraged in moderation by many generations of our family. I remember many afternoons spent exploring the river valley with my dad or grandma, following the unmistakable scent of wild mint. It is a special treat to use this herb in the kitchen, with its somewhat overpowering flavor evoking many happy memories. I greatly enjoy incorporating wild mint with garlic scapes in a summery garlic butter.

Garlic Scape Pesto

Pesto is a great way to use up the odds and ends of garden greens.
I like to showcase the mild cabbagelike taste of canola leaves,
but you can use spinach, beet leaves, or even carrot tops. Serve it
on pasta or potatoes.

YIELD: ABOUT 2 CUPS

1 cup garlic scapes, cut into small pieces

¼ cup basil

½ cup chopped canola greens, spinach, beet greens, or carrot tops

½ cup grated parmesan cheese

⅓ cup slivered almonds

½ teaspoon lemon juice

½ cup olive oil

1 Place the garlic scapes, basil, and canola greens in a food processor. Pulse until finely chopped.

2 Add the parmesan, almonds, and lemon juice, and pulse to combine. Pour in the oil in small increments and pulse until the desired consistency is reached. Blend until smooth. Adjust the consistency by adding more oil if necessary. Store in the refrigerator for up to 5 days or freeze for up to 6 months.

Scape Pesto Spaghetti

Spaghetti squash has been a longtime favorite in our household;
it is so easy to use as a lighter substitute for pasta. With vegetables
from out of the garden, this "pasta" dish has a very summery feel.

YIELD: 4 SERVINGS

1 medium-sized spaghetti squash

1 teaspoon butter

1 small zucchini, sliced

1 cup asparagus, trimmed and cut into 2-inch pieces

1 cup cooked and shredded chicken

¼ cup Garlic Scape Pesto (page 67)

¼ cup cherry tomatoes, halved

1 tablespoon chive blossoms (about 1 flower separated into individual florets)

Flake salt

1 Preheat the oven to 375°F (190°C).

2 Split the squash in half and scoop out and discard the stringy seeds. Place the halves upside down in a baking dish. Cover with foil and bake for 1 hour, until the squash is tender when pierced with a fork.

3 Meanwhile, melt the butter in a large skillet over medium-high heat. Add the zucchini and asparagus and cook until tender but still a little crunchy, 6 to 8 minutes. Be careful not to overcook the vegetables.

4 Scoop out the squash using a fork so that tendrils similar to spaghetti come away.

5 Add the squash and chicken to the vegetable skillet. Stir in the pesto until well combined. Mix in the tomatoes.

6 Garnish with chive blossoms and flake salt.

Beer-Battered Zucchini Blossoms *with* Garlic Scape Filling

Stuffed zucchini blossoms are a garden delicacy, especially when cooked with a scrumptious garlic and lavender cheese filling! They can be a bit delicate to work with, but the result is well worth the extra effort.

YIELD: 6 SMALL SERVINGS

½ cup goat cheese

2 tablespoons finely minced garlic scapes

1 teaspoon culinary lavender buds, crushed

1 teaspoon freshly ground black pepper

¾ cup beer

½ cup all-purpose flour

1 teaspoon garlic powder (homemade, see page 212, or store-bought)

6 female zucchini blossoms (with young zucchini still attached)

Vegetable oil, for frying

1 Create the filling by combining the cheese, garlic scapes, lavender, and pepper in a small mixing bowl.

2 Make the batter by combining the beer, flour, and garlic powder in a medium mixing bowl. The batter should be runny. If it's not, add water 1 teaspoon at a time.

3 Prepare the blossoms by cutting a lengthwise slit on the side of the flower and gently cleaning away any dirt inside. Fill each blossom with 1 tablespoon of the filling. Twist the ends to seal.

continued on page 72

Beer-Battered Zucchini Blossoms *with* Garlic Scape Filling *continued*

4 Heat about 1 inch of oil in a medium skillet over medium heat until it reaches 350°F (180°C).

5 Gently dip each filled blossom in the batter. Carefully place each in the oil. Cook for 2 to 3 minutes on one side, then flip and cook for 3 minutes longer. Place briefly on a paper towel–lined plate to drain, and serve warm.

Garlic Scape Cornbread Muffins

Most of us are well acquainted with jalapeño cornbread, but have you ever tried one made with garlic scapes? This basic sweet cornbread muffin recipe can easily be dressed up by adding sun-dried tomatoes or sharp cheddar cheese. I love being able to make and freeze a big batch ahead of time to serve for breakfasts throughout the busy summer season.

YIELD: 12 SERVINGS

1 cup all-purpose flour

¾ cup coarse cornmeal

¼ cup sugar

2 teaspoons baking powder

¼ teaspoon salt

1 cup milk

4 tablespoons butter, melted

2 eggs

½ cup garlic scapes, finely minced

1 Preheat the oven to 425°F (220°C). Line a 12-cup muffin pan with paper liners.

2 Combine the flour, cornmeal, sugar, baking powder, and salt in a large mixing bowl.

3 Whisk together the milk, butter, and eggs in a medium bowl. Pour into the flour mixture, then add the garlic scapes. Stir with a spoon until just combined.

4 Fill each prepared muffin cup three-quarters full of cornbread mixture. Bake for 15 to 20 minutes, until a toothpick inserted in the center of a muffin comes out clean.

Roasted Garlic Scape
and Tomato Soup

This soup is packed with rich flavors! Make in winter with tomatoes and garlic scapes from the freezer and it will warm you from the inside out.

YIELD: 4 SERVINGS

2 pounds tomatoes

2 tablespoons olive oil

1 pound garlic scapes, broken into small pieces

1 medium-sized onion, diced

2 cups chicken stock

2 tablespoons finely cut fresh basil

½ cup heavy cream

Salt and freshly ground black pepper

Garlic Scape Pesto (page 67), for garnish

Garlic Scape Croutons (page 118), for garnish (optional)

1 Preheat the oven to 375°F (190°C).

2 Place the tomatoes on a rimmed baking sheet and sprinkle with 1 tablespoon of the oil. Roast for 30 to 35 minutes, until the skins pucker and the tomatoes can be easily squeezed.

3 Heat the remaining 1 tablespoon oil in a soup pot. Add the garlic scapes and onion. Cook until the onion becomes translucent, 8 to 10 minutes.

4 Gently squeeze each roasted tomato so that the pulp falls into the soup pot. Discard the skins.

5 Add the stock and basil to the pot, bring to a boil, and then lower the heat and simmer for 10 to 15 minutes, until the soup is aromatic and slightly darker in color.

6 Slowly stir in the cream. Season to taste with salt and pepper.

7 Using an immersion blender, blend the soup until smooth.

8 Garnish each serving with a swirl of pesto and with croutons, if desired.

Garlic Scape Refrigerator Pickles

A quick-pickle recipe saves so much time, especially when the summer months get busy and I would much rather spend my time outside in the sunshine than inside making pickles. These pickled scapes are not processed and therefore must be stored in the refrigerator. They are wonderful on top of salads and burgers or as a garnish for a garlicky cocktail.

YIELD: 1 PINT

1 teaspoon dill seeds

1 pound garlic scapes

1 cup water

1 cup distilled white vinegar

4 teaspoons salt

4 teaspoons sugar

1 Wash and sanitize a pint canning jar. (I boil mine for 15 minutes.)

2 Place the dill seeds in the jar. Arrange the garlic scapes to fit inside the jar, whether by curling the scapes and layering them or by cutting them into bite-size pieces. You can leave the tips on.

3 Stir together the water, vinegar, salt, and sugar in a small saucepan over medium heat. Cook until the salt and sugar are dissolved and the mixture begins to boil, 10 to 12 minutes.

4 Pour the hot brine over the garlic scapes in the jar, leaving ½ inch of headspace at the top of the jar.

5 Screw on the lid and let the jar sit, undisturbed, until completely cool. Store in the refrigerator for up to 4 weeks.

Fresh Garlic Scape Salsa

Fresh salsa is so flavorful and enticing. The scapes add a fun garlicky twist to this garden classic, creating the perfect blend of fresh ingredients and lime. The best part is that you can customize this salsa to your own preference—add more jalapeños for a spicier version, or skip the cilantro if you don't care for it. If you are able to, prepare this salsa ahead of time to let the flavors meld. Enjoy it with tortilla chips.

YIELD: ABOUT 2 CUPS

- 5 paste tomatoes, diced
- ½ cup minced white onion
- ½ cup garlic scapes, finely chopped
- 1 jalapeño, seeded and finely chopped
- ½ teaspoon salt
- Juice of 1 small lime (1 tablespoon of juice)
- ½ cup fresh cilantro, finely chopped

1 Combine the tomatoes, onion, garlic scapes, and jalapeño in a medium bowl. Sprinkle with the salt. Add the lime juice and cilantro and stir to mix thoroughly.

2 Let sit in the refrigerator for at least 30 minutes before serving. Store for up to 3 days.

Roasted Garlic Flowers

The cluster of bulbils within the scape, also called the flower, is edible.
Cook the garlic flowers in the same way you would prepare garlic confit.
Use them as a striking addition to charcuterie boards or as a garnish
on steaks and mashed potatoes for a garlic-themed dinner.

YIELD: 8-10 SERVINGS

8-10 garlic flowers

2 fresh rosemary sprigs

1 fresh thyme sprig

1 bay leaf

1 cup olive oil

1 Preheat the oven to 300°F (150°C).

2 Place the flowers, still intact, in a small baking dish. Add the rosemary, thyme, and bay leaf. Pour the oil over all.

3 Roast for about 90 minutes, until softened and lightly browned.

black garlic recipes

Black garlic is a beautiful, heat-aged ingredient with dramatic flair. The dark bulbs are not grown that way; they're actually fresh bulbs that have been slowly fermented, transforming both the flavor and color of the garlic.

The process originated in Korea centuries ago. A consistent heat is applied over many days in a humidity-controlled environment, resulting in the caramelization of the natural sugars within the bulbs. This caramelization is called the Maillard reaction, named for a French chemist; it describes the reaction of amino acids and simple sugars that causes the cloves to shift to the darker shade. In traditional fermentation chambers, the Maillard process could take several months, but modern technology has sped the process up somewhat with dedicated black garlic machines that heat similarly to rice cookers. The inky colored cloves are loaded with more than twice the amount of antioxidants and taste somewhat sweet, with hints of licorice and balsamic vinegar. The overall flavor effect is quite impressive, making black garlic a powerful addition to any recipe.

USING BLACK GARLIC

You can use black garlic in place of regular garlic, although it does have a distinctive flavor—a strong umami essence with a slightly milder garlicky taste. Gone is the fiery punch of fresh garlic, and in its place are notes of molasses and caramel, proving there can be a softer side to the cloves. Aside from the antioxidant boost, the best thing about black garlic is that it can be both savory and sweet. Because of that, you can enjoy black garlic raw, on its own, or paired deliciously with most meats, sharp cheeses, mushrooms, and even chocolate. The unique sweet flavor makes black garlic fun to work with, giving you ample opportunities to create the unexpected, like chocolate chip cookies. You will notice that the cloves are slightly soft and somewhat squishy, making them easy to chop or mash, whichever the recipe requires.

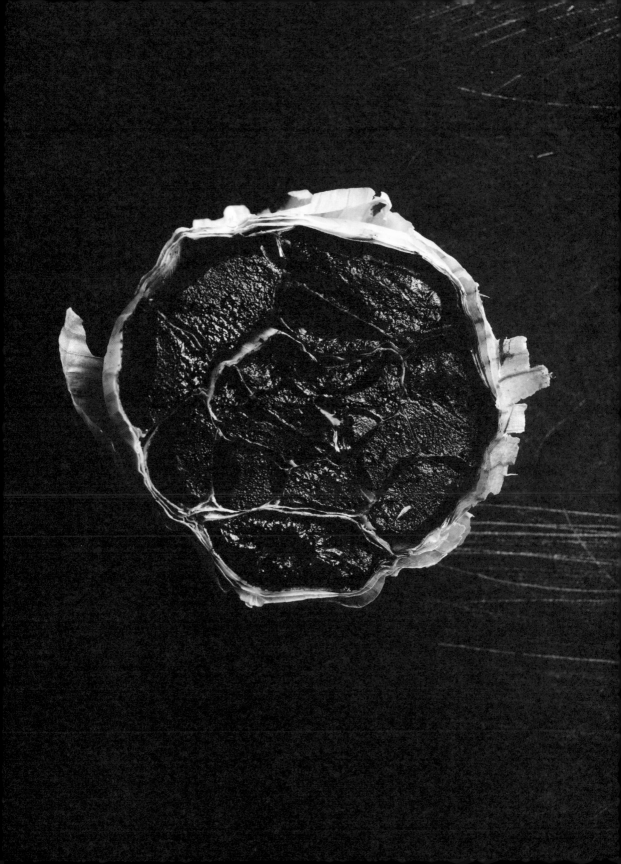

Black Garlic–Maple Butter

This is a sweeter version of a classic garlic butter that can be enjoyed served on fresh bread or even waffles.

YIELD: ½ CUP OR 4 SERVINGS

- 1 black garlic bulb, peeled
- ½ cup (1 stick) unsalted butter, softened
- 2 tablespoons maple syrup
- Pinch of salt

1 Using a fork, mash the black garlic cloves into a paste.

2 Combine the mashed garlic, butter, maple syrup, and salt in a small bowl. Using an electric mixer on low speed, whip the mixture until it is thoroughly combined.

3 Scrape the mixture onto parchment paper and form into a log.

4 Chill for at least 30 minutes to allow the flavors to meld. Store in the refrigerator for up to 2 weeks, or cut into smaller portions to freeze.

Black Garlic Simple Syrup

Add a small spoonful to flavor lemonades, hot chocolate, or cocktails. Or use in lieu of vanilla extract for baked goods.

YIELD: ABOUT ½ CUP

½ cup water

½ cup packed brown sugar

2 black garlic cloves, peeled and chopped

1 Combine the water and sugar in a small saucepan. Stir until the sugar fully dissolves.

2 Add the garlic and bring to a boil. Reduce the heat and simmer until the syrup thickens, 5 to 7 minutes.

3 Strain through a fine-mesh strainer and discard the garlic pieces. Store the syrup in an airtight container in the refrigerator for up to 2 weeks.

Black Garlic Breakfast Toast

A hearty breakfast is an essential start to the day. This breakfast toast with slices of black garlic is quick and easy to make.

YIELD: 2 SERVINGS

- 1 avocado
- 2 slices sourdough toast
- 2 black garlic cloves, peeled and thinly sliced
- 6 thin slices red onion
- Vinegar
- 2 eggs
- 1 tablespoon fresh cilantro, finely chopped
- 4 slices lox-style cold smoked salmon (optional)

1. Mash the avocado and spread evenly onto the 2 pieces of toast. Arrange the garlic and onion slices evenly between the 2 toasts.

2. Add a few drops of vinegar to a pan of water. Bring the pan to a boil, then reduce the heat to a good simmer. Crack each egg into its own small bowl. Swirl the water and gently pour the eggs, one at a time, into the water. Put the lid on the pan and poach the eggs for 4 minutes for medium yolks. Remove the eggs with a slotted spoon, let the water drip off, and set one on each toast.

3. Top with cilantro. Add 2 slices of salmon to each toast, if desired.

Black Garlic Banana Bread

A good banana bread reminds me so much of the comforts of home. There is much debate over whether the loaves should include raisins or chocolate chips, but I prefer raisins because that is how my mom makes hers. The black garlic gives this bread an earthy, almost nutty element that blends beautifully with the bananas.

YIELD: 1 LOAF

½ cup (1 stick) butter or margarine, plus more for the pan

1 cup sugar

¼ cup black garlic (about 2 bulbs), peeled and mashed with a fork

2 eggs, well beaten

1 cup mashed very ripe bananas

1¾ cups all-purpose flour

1 teaspoon baking soda

½ teaspoon baking powder

½ teaspoon salt

½ cup raisins or chocolate chips

1 Preheat the oven to 350°F (180°C). Butter a 9- by 5-inch loaf pan.

2 Cream the sugar, butter, and garlic in a large mixing bowl, either by hand or with an electric mixer. Add the eggs and beat the mixture until smooth. Blend in the bananas.

3 Stir together the flour, baking soda, baking powder, salt, and raisins in a small mixing bowl. Add to the banana mixture, stirring only enough to moisten. Transfer to the prepared loaf pan.

4 Bake for 1 hour, until a toothpick inserted in the center comes out clean. Let stand for 10 minutes, then remove from the pan and place on a wire rack to cool. Eat within 5 days.

Bacon-Wrapped Dates *with* Black Garlic–Cream Cheese Filling

Bacon-wrapped dates are always a big hit at potlucks. They have a pleasing blend of sweet and savory tones, making them the perfect appetizer for your next dinner party.

YIELD: 20 DATES

20 Medjool dates

½ cup cream cheese, softened

2 black garlic cloves, peeled

10 strips bacon, halved

1 Preheat the oven to 400°F (200°C). Line a baking sheet with parchment paper.

2 Carefully slice the dates lengthwise on one side to remove the pit, but do not cut the whole way through.

3 Mix the cream cheese and garlic together in a small bowl. Spoon into each date.

4 Wrap each date in a piece of bacon and place on the prepared baking sheet.

5 Bake for 20 minutes, until the bacon is crispy.

Roasted Carrots *with* Black Garlic Glaze

Roasted vegetables turn a simple meal into an enlightened one. The depth of flavor and sweetness in these carrots is further bolstered by that of the black garlic. This will make a memorable side dish for all your special occasions.

YIELD: 4 SERVINGS

1 pound carrots

1 tablespoon Dijon mustard

2 tablespoons olive oil

1 black garlic clove, peeled

1 garlic clove, peeled

1 teaspoon balsamic vinegar

1 teaspoon honey

¼ teaspoon freshly ground black pepper

¼ teaspoon flake salt

1 Preheat the oven to 425°F (220°C).

2 Peel the carrots and cut any large chunks into medium-sized pieces. Small carrots can be left whole.

3 Combine the mustard, oil, garlics, vinegar, honey, and pepper in a food processor. Pulse until smooth.

4 Place the carrots in a large bowl and pour half of the mustard mixture over them, saving the other half for later. Toss the carrots to evenly coat. Spread in a single layer on a baking sheet.

5 Bake for 20 minutes, stirring occasionally, until the carrots are fork-tender. Remove from the oven, drizzle with the remaining mustard mixture, and roast for 5 minutes longer.

6 Sprinkle with flake salt before serving.

Black Garlic
Mac *and* Cheese

*Baked mac and cheese was a staple on my childhood table. As my
tastes evolved to favor more complexity, I experimented with new
foods but still held a deep appreciation for the basics. Here the umami
flavor of black garlic complements the mushrooms and smoked cheese,
making this an enjoyable, grown-up version of a favorite dish.*

2 cups elbow macaroni

4 tablespoons butter

1 tablespoon chopped onion

¼ cup chopped mushrooms

¼ cup all-purpose flour

½ teaspoon garlic powder (homemade, see page 212, or store-bought)

¼ teaspoon salt

¼ teaspoon freshly ground black pepper

2 cups milk

½ cup shredded cheddar cheese

½ cup shredded smoked Gouda cheese

2 tablespoons diced black garlic

½ cup panko breadcrumbs

1 tablespoon truffle oil

1 Bring a large pot of water to a boil and cook the macaroni according to the package directions. Drain and set aside.

2 Preheat the oven to 375°F (190°C). Grease a 9-inch square casserole dish.

3 Melt the butter in a skillet over medium heat. Add the onion and mushrooms, and cook slowly, stirring often, until the onion is translucent, about 10 minutes. Stir in the flour, garlic powder, salt, and pepper until well combined.

4 Gradually stir in the milk. Add the cheeses and continue stirring until all the cheese is melted, then stir in the macaroni and garlic. Stir until the pasta is well coated. Pour into the prepared casserole dish. Top with the breadcrumbs. Drizzle evenly with the oil.

5 Bake, covered, for 30 minutes. Remove the cover and bake for 3 to 5 minutes longer, until the breadcrumbs have browned slightly.

Black Garlic–Chocolate Chip Cookies

Chocolate and black garlic might be thought of as an unlikely pair. But when put together, the black garlic draws out the richness of the chocolate. These are not your usual chocolate chip cookies, but they are incredibly decadent and very tasty.

YIELD: 24 COOKIES

1 cup all-purpose flour

½ teaspoon salt

½ teaspoon baking soda

½ cup (1 stick) butter, softened

½ cup granulated sugar

¼ cup packed brown sugar

1 egg

1 (6-ounce) package semisweet chocolate chips

2 black garlic bulbs, peeled and cut into small pieces

1 Preheat the oven to 375°F (190°C).

2 Sift together the flour, salt, and baking soda into a small bowl.

3 Cream together the butter, sugars, and egg in a large mixing bowl, using a stand mixer. Stir in the chocolate chips and garlic. Add the flour mixture and mix until combined.

4 Drop the batter by teaspoonfuls, about 1 inch apart, on ungreased baking sheets.

5 Bake for 8 to 10 minutes, until edges are browned. Let stand for 30 seconds before transferring the cookies to wire racks.

Black Garlic *and* Caramel Mini Cheesecakes

I love the surprise and awe that accompanies this cheesecake. With a sweet, nutty finish, this heavenly combination of black garlic with cream cheese will leave guests begging for more. They will never guess the secret ingredient—black garlic!

YIELD: 12 SERVINGS

for the crust

- 1 cup graham cracker crumbs
- ¼ cup granulated sugar
- 4 tablespoons unsalted butter, melted

for the filling

- 2 (8-ounce) packages cream cheese, softened
- ⅓ cup sour cream, at room temperature
- ½ cup granulated sugar
- ¼ cup black garlic (roughly 2 bulbs), peeled and mashed with a fork
- 2 eggs

for the topping

- 1 cup heavy cream
- ¼ cup confectioners' sugar
- ½ teaspoon vanilla extract
- Caramel sauce, for serving (optional)

continued on page 104

Black Garlic *and* Caramel Mini Cheesecakes

continued

1   Preheat the oven to 325°F (170°C). Line a 12-cup muffin pan with paper liners. Chill a large mixing bowl for use in step 8.

2   Make the crust: Combine the graham cracker crumbs and granulated sugar in a second large mixing bowl. Add the melted butter and stir to combine. Spoon the crumb mixture into the prepared muffin pan, pressing the mixture firmly into each cup.

3   Bake the crusts for 5 minutes. Remove from the oven and set aside. Leave the oven on.

4   Meanwhile, make the filling: Using an electric mixer on low speed, cream together the cream cheese and sour cream in a large bowl. Add the granulated sugar and garlic and mix to fully combine. Add the eggs, one at a time, and mix the batter until just combined.

5   Scoop the filling into the baked muffin crusts. Fill each cup until nearly full.

6   Bake for 20 to 25 minutes, until the tops of the cheesecakes are set.

7   Let the cheesecakes cool in the pan for at least 1 hour. Chill in the refrigerator for at least 6 hours. The cheesecakes will continue to firm up as they cool.

8   Just before serving, make the topping: Combine the heavy cream, confectioners' sugar, and vanilla in the chilled mixing bowl. Mix on medium-high speed until medium-stiff peaks form, 3 to 4 minutes. Top each cheesecake with a swirl of the topping and drizzle with caramel sauce, if desired.

TIP: Make the cheesecake filling with room-temperature ingredients to prevent cracking.

Black Garlic Chocolates

My mom is known for her homemade chocolates, her kitchen recognized by the alluring aroma of buttery caramel simmering on the stove. It was so fun to combine our two passions and create a recipe for these black garlic–cream fondant chocolates. They were a big hit, and our customers raved about them.

YIELD: ABOUT 5 DOZEN CHOCOLATES

2 tablespoons butter, plus more to coat the pot

1½ cups heavy cream

4 cups sugar

6 tablespoons white corn syrup

Pinch of table salt

1 teaspoon vanilla extract

¼ cup black garlic (about 2 bulbs), peeled and mashed with a fork

5 cups dark chocolate wafers

Sea salt (optional)

1 Butter a large heavy-bottomed pot, making sure to coat the sides to prevent the fondant from rising during cooking. Do not skip this step or you will have a sticky mess! Prepare an ice-water bath large enough to hold the pot; set aside.

2 Place the pot over medium-high heat. Pour in the cream and scald (cook, stirring frequently, until steam begins to rise).

3 Stir in the sugar, corn syrup, and salt. Stir continuously over medium heat until the sugar dissolves. Bring the mixture to a boil and cook until it registers 232°F (111°C) on a candy thermometer, just above the soft ball stage, 25 to 30 minutes.

4 Remove the pot from the heat. Add the 2 tablespoons butter, vanilla, and garlic, but do not stir. Immediately transfer the pot to the prepared ice-water bath to rapidly cool.

5 Once the fondant has cooled, pour it onto a clean work surface
and knead until it's thick, working in the garlic as you go.
This process can take quite a long time—at least 35 minutes.
Be patient and keep working the fondant back and forth.

6 Once the fondant can hold its shape, place it in a bowl, cover,
and chill for at least 1 hour.

7 Scoop spoonfuls of fondant to form ½-inch pucks and place
on a cookie sheet lined with waxed paper. Keep cool until ready
to dip.

8 Working in small batches, slowly melt some of the chocolate
wafers in a shallow pan over low heat, stirring constantly to
prevent burning. Remove from the heat once melted. Repeat this
step when more chocolate is needed.

9 Dip the fondant pucks in the melted chocolate and place back on
the waxed paper to dry. Sprinkle sea salt over the top, if desired.

garlic powder recipes

Like any other garden vegetable, fresh garlic or garlic scapes won't last forever. Making your own ground garlic powder allows you to utilize your crop year-round, without sacrificing flavor. You can create aromatic blends with other dried herbs to be used later in other dishes, or substitute freshly ground garlic powder for fresh cloves when none are available. (See page 212 for instructions on making garlic powder from fresh bulbs.)

Rosemary Garlic Salt

Our garlic salt is made with a ratio of two parts garlic to three parts salt. Have fun and experiment with other flavors by adding different dried herbs. I love the way rosemary lends an extra pop to this version.

YIELD: 2 CUPS

1 cup table salt

⅔ cup freshly ground garlic powder (see page 212)

⅓ cup dried rosemary

1 Mix the salt, garlic powder, and rosemary together in a small bowl until well blended.

2 Store in an airtight container for up to 1 year.

Garlic Scape Pepper

This is one of our most popular garlic scape products. It is incredibly simple to make, with just two ingredients, but it packs a punch of flavor. Enjoy it on steaks, ribs, or roasted vegetables.

YIELD: ½ CUP

¼ cup dehydrated garlic scapes, finely ground (see page 199)

¼ cup freshly ground black pepper

Combine the scapes and pepper in a small bowl. Store in an airtight container or spice jar for up to 1 year.

Savory Shortbread Cookies

Whoever said shortbread was only meant to be sweet was completely wrong. This recipe has been adapted from my grandmother's, now with the addition of garlic. The richness of the butter in the shortbread complements the herbed garlic component, giving these cookies a wow factor for any charcuterie board or cookie exchange.

YIELD: 24 COOKIES

1	pound butter, softened
1	teaspoon freshly ground garlic powder (see page 212)
¼	teaspoon dried thyme
¼	teaspoon freshly ground black pepper
1	cup confectioners' sugar
3¼	cups all-purpose flour
½	cup rice flour
½	teaspoon baking powder
3	tablespoons cornstarch
½	teaspoon salt

1 Combine the butter, garlic powder, thyme, and pepper in a large mixing bowl, using an electric mixer. Cover and let sit at room temperature for at least 2 hours to allow the flavors to meld.

2 Preheat the oven to 300°F (150°C).

3 Add the sugar to the butter mixture and blend until light and fluffy.

4 Sift together the flours, baking powder, cornstarch, and salt. Add to the butter mixture and mix until crumbly. On a lightly floured work surface, knead the dough until it's smooth and soft.

5 Roll the dough into a log, then cut into ¼-inch slices and place on an ungreased baking sheet.

6 Bake for 25 to 30 minutes, until cookies are lightly golden across the top.

Grandma's Garlic Cabbage Slaw

Grandma's kitchen was filled with great food and big hugs. Her cabbage slaw is still my go-to salad for any meal. The apple and carrot add just a hint of sweetness.

YIELD: 4 SERVINGS

for the slaw

3 cups shredded cabbage

1 cup chopped celery

1 large carrot, shredded

¼ cup chopped onion

1 unpeeled apple, cored and chopped

for the dressing

5 tablespoons distilled white vinegar

¼ cup sugar

1 teaspoon garlic powder

1 tablespoon hot water

¼ cup whole milk

1 Make the slaw: Combine the cabbage, celery, carrot, onion, and apple in a large salad bowl. Set aside.

2 Make the dressing: Combine the vinegar, sugar, and garlic powder in a small bowl. Stir well. Add the hot water and stir again. Gradually add the milk, stirring continuously.

3 Pour the dressing over the slaw. Cover and refrigerate at least 1 hour before serving.

Rosemary–Garlic Scape Popcorn

Popcorn is a must when it comes to snacking on the farm, and I've always preferred salty over sweet. My favorite combo is freshly popped popcorn sprinkled with garlic, robust herbs, and cheese. The garlic scape powder brings a festive element to a familiar salty snack, easy to take with you to the garden or on the road.

YIELD: 10 CUPS POPPED POPCORN

½ cup popcorn kernels

4 tablespoons butter

1 teaspoon garlic scape powder (see page 199)

1 teaspoon finely chopped fresh rosemary

Salt

¼ cup shredded white cheddar cheese (optional)

1 Pop the kernels according to your popper's instructions (we use a stovetop popper). Empty the popped kernels into a large bowl.

2 Meanwhile, melt the butter in a small pan over medium heat. Mix in the scape powder and rosemary.

3 Pour the butter mixture over the popcorn. Toss to coat evenly. Add a pinch of salt, or more to taste, and the cheese, if using, then toss to mix.

Garlic Scape Croutons

This is a great recipe to use up any leftover or slightly stale bread. Garlic scapes give the croutons a unique flavor, perfect to top any salad or tomato soup.

YIELD: 4 CUPS

4 cups small cubes of sourdough bread

4 tablespoons butter

1 teaspoon garlic scape powder (see page 199)

2 teaspoons grated parmesan cheese

1 Preheat the oven to 350°F (180°C). Line a baking sheet with parchment paper.

2 Place the bread cubes in a large bowl.

3 Melt the butter in a small pan over medium heat and stir in the scape powder. Pour the mixture over the bread. Toss with your hands until the bread is evenly coated.

4 Spread the cubes evenly on the prepared baking sheet and bake for 10 minutes. Remove the sheet from the oven, then sprinkle the parmesan on the croutons and stir. Bake for 10 minutes longer, until the croutons begin to turn golden brown.

Michael

Kaitlyn

Peter

Catherine

Paul

Joanne

3

crafts for garlic gatherings

Garlic is a plant that holds deep meaning. It facilitates camaraderie through bold flavors, intriguing meals, and the pride of a success-ful harvest. The tiny cloves have the ability to focus your cooking and hosting prac-tices, making it an easy ingredient to build an entire event around. Hosting a garlic celebration gives you the freedom to have fun showcasing the bulbs. Beautiful crafts, such as centerpieces or place settings, bol-ster a delicious garlicky meal; eye-catching garlic crowns add an ethereal element for you and your guests; and garlic braids and other storage decorations creatively display your crop. There are countless ways to incorporate garlic into homemade crafts. Garlic is a vegetable with an undeniably bold character and a big heart. No wonder it's to love!

A Garlic Gathering

At the farm we love to celebrate garlic with events that bring people together around the table to enjoy the festive flavor and aroma of our favorite bulbs. It gives us joy to share an appreciation for good food. And we return to that joy again each season through gatherings centered around garlic.

Food nourishes the body, but a meal also nourishes the mind. A meal is meant to be savored with family and friends gathered around the table. Aside from the garlic, the table is really the center of our festivities. At our gatherings, diners who come from near and far are seated at a long, extended table. Some are old friends, some are new.

As guests arrive, they excitedly take in the sheer size of our garlic wall (see page 207), while the tantalizing aroma of roasted garlic draws them in. The table is adorned with boughs of foraged greens accented by brightly colored bulbs and homegrown flowers. Handmade decorations create a unique tablescape, one that invites diners to find their seat by the beautiful bulb place settings. Rich colors associated with the harvest are illuminated by the twinkling lights strung over the table. The overall effect is meant to entice diners to linger—to prolong the meal as the sun slowly dips beneath the horizon.

The evening is full of chatter and meaningful connections. While garlic is most certainly the catalyst that sparks much of the flowing conversation, the discussions vary and cover a wide range of topics. I like to think of these events as hearkening to another time, when European salons facilitated the exchange of ideas as well as food. These salons became a vital part of philosophical movements throughout history. A garlic gathering is an inclusive way for people to come together as equals, regardless of their status.

As the night comes to a close, people leave not only with hearts and bellies full but with new thoughts and ideas seeded in their minds. Sometimes our events include a formal presentation, but even when they don't, the dinners are rife with opportunities for learning as well as socializing. Yes, garlic is undoubtedly the central focus at these types of gatherings, but it is the people who make them so special.

Food nourishes the body, but a meal also nourishes the mind.

There's nothing quite like the taste of barbecued roasted garlic! On our farm, we slow roast the bulbs on a wood-fired grill to further enhance the smoky flavor. The smooth and buttery texture of the bulbs complements the grilled garlic taste and is a wonderful addition to any celebratory dinner.

Host a Garlic-Themed Dinner

Garlic gives us the opportunity to celebrate two distinct harvests: the garlic scapes in summer as well as the bulbs in fall. Each bounty creates completely different table experiences, with menus catered to include fresh ingredients associated with the season. Each fresh crop is reason enough to come together and feast on the unmistakable flavor of garlic.

Celebrate the Bulb Harvest with a Fall Feast

Garlic-themed dinners can be as simple or as elaborate as you make them, but overall they present some of the most unique ways to showcase the powerful flavors offered by this plant. Cherish the harvest season by sourcing local ingredients to add to the festive meal. Invite all of the garlic lovers you know, and explore the culinary adventures that garlic holds. Create a

What better way to demonstrate the incredible flavor of locally produced ingredients than with a hearty meal?

cozy atmosphere with flickering candles, and offer your guests flannel blankets to keep them warm while they dine under leaves' autumn colors.

Impress your dinner guests with recipes they wouldn't expect to have garlic as an ingredient, such as Barbecued Roasted Garlic (page 55), Bacon-Wrapped Dates with Black Garlic–Cream Cheese Filling (page 95), and Black Garlic and Caramel Mini Cheesecakes (page 103).

Decorate your table to feature the rich earth tones associated with autumn, enhanced by beautiful arrangements of locally grown flowers and brightly hued garlic cloves. If you don't grow a garlic crop of your own, consider inviting a local gardener or garlic producer to join in on the festivities and share information about cultivation. The most important part is to make the event fun!

Serve Up Garlic Scapes at a Summer Supper

Try hosting a garlic scape dinner. Plan the event to occur when the garden is lush and the garlic scapes are plentiful. This is the perfect opportunity for a backyard feast! Treat your guests to an intimate dinner served within a tranquil garden oasis.

Garlic scapes are in season when the garden is ripe with fresh vegetables. Try to incorporate seasonal ingredients that help showcase the iconic garlic curls. Consider serving Beer-Battered Zucchini Blossoms with Garlic Scape Filling (page 71), Grilled Garlic Scapes (page 63) to accompany barbecued steaks, and a festive garlic butter board (see page 133).

Decorate the Dinner Table

Use garlic bulbs as creative decorations to draw attention to the star ingredient of your dinner. A garlic bulb's violet stripes make it as beautiful as it is appetizing. Adding seasonal florals helps create an inviting aesthetic for guests. Don't worry about being wasteful, as all the garlic can later be used in the kitchen after the dinner is finished.

Decorate the table with beautiful bouquets that combine the attractive garlic bulbil "flowers" with garden florals. Vegetable bouquets are also popular, offering varying textures from delicate dill flowers to deeply ridged Savoy cabbage leaves. Artichokes, with their scaled globes, are striking when added to a bouquet of blooms. Take a quick walk through the garden to find something that inspires you.

Adding seasonal florals helps create an inviting aesthetic for guests to gather around.

Scape *and* Mixed Flower Arrangements

The curls of the garlic scapes bring an air of whimsy to this fun bouquet. Garlic scapes that are left on the plant eventually turn woody and somewhat rigid. At that point they can still be dehydrated and coarsely ground— or they could serve as a beautiful addition to a mixed floral arrangement featuring any seasonal flowers.

Clear floral tape or flower frog

Vase

6 stems fresh greens

12–15 stems mixed flowers

1 stem delphinium

12 long-stemmed garlic scapes

3 stems filler flowers (baby's breath or statice)

1 Use the tape to create a grid over the mouth of the vase. Alternatively, insert a flower frog in the vase.

2 Arrange 4 stems of the greens as the base, with 1 stem on each side of the vase.

3 Place 4 stems of mixed flowers at the base. Set the delphinium in the center of the arrangement, keeping its stem long enough to achieve the overall desired height of the bouquet.

4 Continue to add mixed florals evenly until the bouquet is nearly full. Insert the remaining 2 stems of greens in the center of the bouquet.

5 Add in the garlic scapes to fill any gaps. Use the filler flowers to finish.

Festive Butter Board

Butter boards are an exciting new take on a traditional bread-and-butter platter. They are easy to put together and are an affordable alternative to charcuterie spreads. The colorful display of butter is a real showstopper! Each board is completely unique, with customizable ingredients. This recipe is a base structure to follow when making a butter board. Serve with fresh bread.

1 cup garlic butter, softened (see pages 58, 64, and 87)

2 teaspoons chopped edible flowers

1 teaspoon chopped fresh herbs

Zest from 1 lemon or other citrus fruit

Honey

optional ingredients

Pumpkin seeds

Roasted garlic cloves

Prosciutto

Almond slivers

Cracked black pepper

Figs

1 Liberally spread the butter onto a serving platter.

2 Sprinkle the edible flowers and herbs evenly across the spread. Add any optional ingredients, if using. Top with the zest and drizzle with some honey.

Garlic Bulb Place Settings

This is where the differences in garlic varieties readily become apparent. For example, 'Tibetan' garlic cloves shine with the prettiest shade of pink, whereas the 'Persian Star' garlic cloves are red with slight streaks of yellow. Regardless of the variety you use, these place settings provide an eye-catching way to display your guests' names.

1 garlic bulb per guest

Pieces of card stock, roughly 1½ × 2½ inches each

1 Trim the neck of a garlic bulb to be level with the tips of the cloves.

2 Gently peel back the paper layers of the bulb so that the hulls of the cloves are visible. Be careful not to break the cloves off.

3 Neatly write each guest's name on a piece of card stock.

4 Attach the name tag to the peeled bulb by gently nestling it between the cloves.

Garlic, Herb, *and* Sunflower Table Runner

It's no surprise that fresh, live table runners have been popular for years. They are a lovely way to add a natural element to your tabletop. This design bears in mind the significance of the herbs used: garlic for protection, rosemary for good health, and thyme for courage. The instructions are for a six-foot table (with diners seated on both sides and one at each end); adjust accordingly if your table is longer.

SILVER WILLOW

Silver willow, also known as wolf willow, grows wild on our farm. Its leaves hold a shimmery, silvery green hue. In spring, tiny yellow flowers open that emit a sweet, lilylike scent. When making crafts, I often select willow as a green base because it dries well. Eucalyptus would work as an appropriate substitute.

30–35 silver willow branches, each no more than 2 feet long

6–8 rosemary sprigs

6–8 thyme sprigs

Floral wire

5 sunflowers

5–8 garlic bulbs of varying sizes, cleaned, with 3-inch stems

1 Gather 5 silver willow branches together in a bundle. Layer in some rosemary and thyme sprigs. Using a continuous piece of floral wire, twist the wire around the base of the bundle.

continued on page 138

2, 3

4

continued from page 137

2   Keep adding silver willow branches and herbs until the
     desired fullness is achieved, continuing to twist wire around
     the whole bundle each time greenery is added.

3   Repeat steps 1 and 2 until you've reached the desired length.
     Lay the runner flat on the table.

4   Next, arrange 1 sunflower with a garlic bulb as if you were
     making a boutonniere. Join the two by wrapping the stems
     with floral wire. Repeat with the remaining flowers and garlic
     bulbs, creating slightly different combinations.

5   Gently insert the sunflower–garlic bundles evenly along the
     runner.

Illuminated Garlic Centerpiece

This centerpiece uses a double vase to create a gorgeous display of garlic cloves. The smaller vase slips inside the larger one, leaving a large gap in which the garlic will "shine."

3-inch-diameter straight-sided vase

6-inch-diameter straight-sided vase

8–10 garlic bulbs

Small battery-operated candle (see Note)

1 Set the smaller vase inside the larger one.

2 Crack the garlic bulbs and separate the cloves. Be careful not to peel the cloves, as you want the outer papers intact.

3 Fill the gap between the vases with the cloves.

4 Place the candle inside the inner vase.

NOTE: While the flickering flame of a real candle creates a beautiful ambience, it can also cause the garlic to overheat. Choose a battery-operated candle instead.

HOW WE CELEBRATE GARLIC AT THE FARM

On our farm we show our love for growing garlic by sharing it with those around us. Our main intent is to create an open dialogue for prospective growers of all walks of life. From fellow farm producers to backyard enthusiasts, a collective knowledge helps instill a deep-seated appreciation for the flavor-packed bulbs.

We further that understanding by finding new approaches to the usual garlic powders and seasonings and creating lively products to share with our customers. Our passion for locally grown, wholesome food brings forth exciting new recipes that allow anyone to re-create the same celebrations at home. We hope to make the love of garlic accessible for everybody, whether in rural settings or urban dwellings, through a true farm-to-table experience.

At the heart of it all is the strong feeling of community. Where I come from, that means having unwavering support from the people who surround you. In my area, we show up for each other. We fight fires together, we grieve together, we celebrate new beginnings for each other, and we gather together to share in each other's success. Our neighbors help us commemorate a bountiful garlic harvest, and I am so grateful to be able to share it with them!

Wear Garlic in a Crown

When I was a little girl, my grandma wove rings of golden dandelions for my sister and me to wear traipsing around the garden. While garlic crowns certainly are different, they still hold a familiar, magical feeling! The inspiration behind these crowns stemmed from my own logo, which depicts a goddess wearing a crown of garlic with flowers from my garden, barley from our grain fields, and silver willow branches from the local riverbanks.

Garlic crowns are fun to make and are a great addition to your crafting repertoire. Perhaps you are hosting a garlic dinner, or maybe you want to make a splash at the next garlic festival. Whatever your reason, keep these beautiful headbands in mind, because you just never know when you may need to wear one!

Garlic Scape Crown

The garlic scapes, with their fairylike tendrils, add extra whimsy to a floral crown. Be gentle as you work with the garlic scapes: Too firm of a grip can accidentally snap the stalks.

	Craft wire (20–22 gauge) or craft willow, for the base
15–20	garlic scapes
	Assorted wildflowers
	Floral tape
	Floral wire

1 Measure the circumference of the head to determine the size crown you would like to make. Cut 2 or 3 strands of wire to the desired length (it's good to add an inch or two to the circumference, then trim off excess) and twist them together to create a sturdy base.

2 Trim the garlic scapes so that their stems are roughly 3 inches in length from the flower bud (if using young scapes) or flower. Set aside the lower section of the stalks to use in the kitchen.

3 Create mini bouquets by combining a garlic scape tip with assorted wildflowers, and wrap the stems of each grouping with floral tape. The number of bouquets needed will depend on how large or small the crown will be, so adjust accordingly.

4 Attach the bouquets to the wire base tightly with floral wire, overlaying bouquets to create a full look, and weave in any stems that stick out.

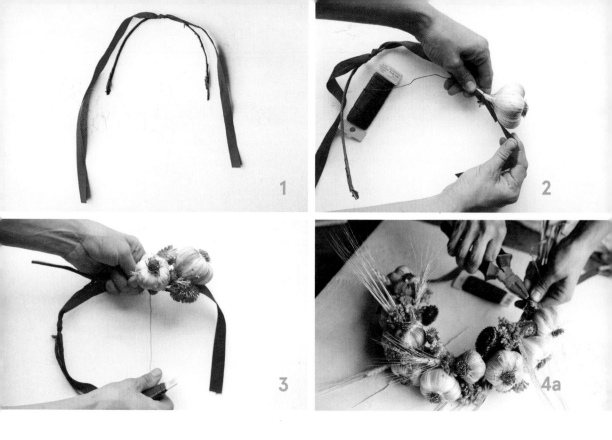

Tied Garlic Crown

Wear a crown full of garlic, bright flowers, and stalks of wheat to feel like a goddess. Creating this as a partial crown, tied at the back with ribbon, makes the considerable weight of the garlic bulbs more tolerable.

Craft willow, for the base

3-foot piece of ribbon

12–15 medium-sized garlic bulbs, cleaned, with roots trimmed and approximately 2-inch stems

Floral wire

8 stems dried strawflowers

5 stems dried statice

7 stalks wheat or barley

4b

4c

5

1 Bend the willow into an arc shape to fit around the front part of your brow. Tie the ribbon to the center of the willow arc base. Each half of the ribbon will lie flat against each side of the arc.

2 Hold one end of the willow base in one hand. Place a garlic bulb at this end with the bulb facing out and the stem facing in, lying against the willow. Hold the ribbon underneath the bulb, and fasten both tightly by wrapping with floral wire. You will fasten both the ribbon and the garlic to the base.

3 Add 2 stems of the florals and the next bulb, facing in the same direction, layering the stems. Wrap with wire around the floral stems and the ribbon to fasten securely.

4 Work your way around the arc, evenly distributing flowers and stalks of wheat between the garlic bulbs and attaching the ribbon on the underside of the base. Finish with flowers to hide the final stem. Trim the stems to line up with the willow base, leaving the extra ribbon as a tie.

5 Wear along the crown of your head and secure with the ribbon in back.

THE GARLIC GODDESS

Goddesses exhibit opposing forces: fierceness and strength alongside grace and beauty. Additionally, a goddess is often thought to hold a deep connection to nature. I couldn't think of any symbol more applicable to my agricultural pursuits.

"Garlic Goddess" originated as a name for a new dip mix; however, the moniker really resonated with me, so it stuck and became my nickname. Over time, the Garlic Goddess became a prominent part of my business logo to celebrate all the women who dared to be different and stepped outside traditional gender roles. She was forged in fire and represents strength in the face of adversity. More important, the Garlic Goddess serves as a reminder that farmers come in all shapes and sizes.

I might not be what comes to mind at first when you think of a farmer, but that is what makes my endeavor extraordinary! As I shifted my career from healthcare back to the farm, I quickly realized how many people doubted my ability to operate machinery or successfully run a business on my own. I am often underestimated because I am a young, short statured woman. Because of that, it should come as no surprise that I long to push against the boundaries of antiquated expectations. Sure, I've made plenty of mistakes along the way, but I have never given up.

With practice I've learned to handle my flaws with kindness and welcome the things that make me different. Finding the source of my passion has given me more confidence than any so-called perfect look ever would. My business, Fifth Gen Gardens, has given me a safe space to cultivate the best version of myself. I aim to continue our family's legacy while promoting the importance of women farmers who embrace their femininity and strength.

To me the message is an important one: Be bold enough to shatter stereotypes. Face adversity with grace. Be authentic. We are all different and unique— let's celebrate that!

Display Dried Bulbs as Decor

Garlic is just as beautiful as it is delicious—no wonder it's an easy addition to favorite home decorations. The striking colors of its paper wrappers, be they purple or pearly white, add dramatic flair, while other natural components, such as herbs and dried florals, provide a pleasing harvest element. Using garlic bulbs in crafts serves a dual purpose—in addition to creating charming displays, you also have a wonderful storage technique.

Hanging a garlic wreath or braid in your kitchen is a great way to keep your favorite ingredient close at hand for when you need it. Be mindful to keep your garlic decor out of direct sunlight to avoid the bulbs spoiling too fast. When it comes time to cook, use your crafted bulbs before digging into other stored bulbs.

Softneck Garlic Braid

Traditional garlic braids are most often made with softneck garlic varieties. When moistened, their soft stems are easy to weave, resulting in beautiful long ropes of bulbs.

12 or more softneck garlic bulbs, cleaned, with stems intact

String

continued on page 152

FRONT

BACK

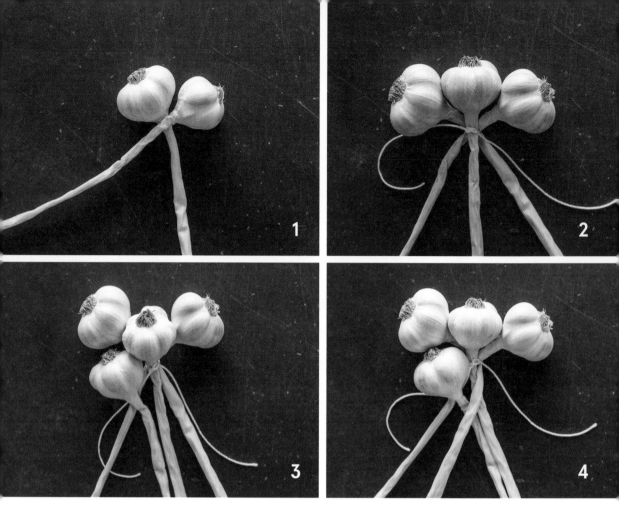

continued from page 151

1 Position 2 garlic bulbs on top of each other so they form an X. The stem of the bulb on the right should cross over the stem of the bulb on the left.

2 Add a third bulb on top of the X, so the stem comes down the middle. Using a small piece of string, tie the three stems together at the place where they overlap.

3 Place a new bulb over the other three on the left side, allowing its stem to overlap down the middle. Note: The new bulb's stem will always go down the middle.

4 Cross the stem and leaves on the right side over to become the middle, starting to create a braid.

5 Place a new bulb on the right side, with its stem and leaves
   down the middle section.

6 Cross the stem on the left side over to the middle.

7 Continue braiding in this pattern until all the bulbs have been
   added. Braid the stems until the end.

8 Tie the end of the stem braid with string. You can also create
   a loop to hang the braid.

1

3

Hardneck Garlic Braid

*While these "braids" do not actually require any interlacing of the stems,
the overall effect is similar to that of a true braid made with softneck garlic.
The bright florals in this project leave you with many options to create
a one-of-a-kind braid. Hardneck garlic braids work best when assembled
with at least 12 bulbs.*

    12 hardneck garlic bulbs, dried and cleaned with stems intact

        Floral wire

     6 stems dried strawflowers

        Ribbon or string

1. Begin with 1 garlic bulb. Arrange 2 additional bulbs, just below it, to form a triangle. Wrap tightly with floral wire.

2. Add another bulb between the last two. Frame it with 2 stems of strawflowers. Wrap tightly with floral wire.

3. Keeping the backside of the braid flat, place 2 more bulbs on either side of the last garlic bulb to form another triangle. Wrap tightly with floral wire. Continue creating the bulb triangles, working in stems of flowers, until all of the bulbs have been used.

4. Tie the end of the "braid" tightly with the ribbon. Create a loop at the back of the braid for hanging.

5. Trim the stems to 6 inches above the final bulbs.

Hand-Tied Garlic Bouquet

My after-school job while in high school was at a local florist shop. When I started making hand-tied garlic bouquets many years later, the happy memories of that job all came rushing back to me. The burst of color in this bouquet brings brightness to dark winters, and the bulbs can be used in the kitchen as needed. I enjoy being able to add my own style and flair to a classic.

7 stalks dried corn tops

9 hardneck garlic bulbs, dried and cleaned but with stems intact

Floral tape

4 stems dried florals, such as strawflowers, statice, or bachelor's buttons

3 stems green filler, such as silver willow, sage, or rosemary

String

Ribbon (optional)

1. Begin with 1 cornstalk. Arrange 3 garlic bulbs around it, and wrap with floral tape about a third of the way down the stems.

2. Add 3 more stalks of corn, as well as 2 stems of flowers and some green filler. Arrange each evenly around the bouquet.

3. Continue building the bouquet by placing 3 more garlic bulbs.

4. Next, add more green filler, allowing some of the leaves to peek out, then place the last 2 stems of flowers.

5. Finish the bouquet with 3 more stalks of corn, as well as the remaining 3 garlic bulbs, being mindful to fill any gaps.

6. Tightly tie the string around the stems to secure the bouquet. Trim the stems to the same length. Add a festive ribbon, if desired.

7. Display your bouquet by either hanging it or placing it in a dry jar. Cut off the bulbs to use in your kitchen when needed.

Garlic Harvest Wreath

The bold purple accents of the garlic bulbs can be a striking addition to this dried floral wreath. Create a unique piece of harvest decor that is not only beautiful to look at but also a functional way to store your garlic! Choose to add seasonal ribbons that can be changed as the year progresses. Wreath hoops are available in a variety of materials; use whatever appeals to you.

1 (12- to 14-inch) wreath hoop

Floral tape

15 stems dried cornstalks

Floral wire

5 stems dried strawflowers

5 garlic bulbs, dried and cleaned with stems intact

3 stems dried statice

2 stems dried sunflowers

10 stems dried green fillers (such as wheat, grasses, herbs)

Ribbon bow (optional)

1   Wrap one-third of the wreath hoop's circumference with floral tape. This is the area where you will add decoration, and the tape helps keep the wreath base from twisting or slipping.

2   Lay the hoop flat on a surface with the taped area closest to you. Place 1 of the cornstalks at the left end of the taped area, pointing to the left on the outside of the hoop with the stalk coming in toward the right. Wrap once with wire where the stalk touches the hoop.

NOTE: Each wreath is one of a kind. Feel free to use any combination of the components. This recipe is simply a guideline to help get you started.

continued on page 160

continued from page 159

3   Add 2 more cornstalks, one to the left of the first, and one to the right. Pick up the hoop in your left hand, holding the added stalks in place, and wrap them tightly to secure to the hoop.

4   Continuing to hold the hoop in your hand, add a stem of strawflowers. Be careful not to break the stem as you wrap the wire. Then place the first garlic bulb and wrap.

5   Keep adding materials around the bottom third of the wreath, holding it in your left hand and wrapping with wire to secure. Maintain the fullness and shape by remembering to add the stalks and filler grasses to both the left and right sides of the arrangement, similar to a braid.

6   When you've reached the end of the taped area, tightly wrap
    a few more times and then fasten the wire. Clean up the stems
    by trimming them to the same length, but be mindful not to
    cut them too short as they will act as a counterbalance to the
    heavier bulbs and stalks. Add a ribbon bow, if desired.

7   Hang the wreath and snip off the garlic bulbs as you need
    them. If you live in a cold climate and wish to hang the wreath
    on your door, be careful not to let the bulbs freeze.

4

PLANT AND GROW

cultivate your own garlic crop

Whether you're a seasoned gardener or a newbie, there are many reasons to grow your own garlic. The plants offer a new perspective on the growing season, as they are most often planted during autumn months when the gardening season has otherwise slowed down. If you've previously known garlic only in the kitchen, adding garlic to your garden plot will better acquaint you with the plant, and you'll get a glimpse of the entire process involved with cultivating those beloved bulbs. Their rapid growth and reliable nature make them easy to grow over and over again. Growing an abundance of garlic also allows you to share the bounty with friends and neighbors. The bulbs are best when shared with the people around you!

The Garlic Plant

Successfully growing garlic requires an intimate understanding of the plant's life stages and parts. While most of us are familiar with garlic cloves from their many uses within the kitchen, not everyone knows that each of these cloves can actually develop into a new whole bulb! Every plant has one goal in life: to reproduce and replicate itself. For garlic, this can be accomplished in one of two ways—by producing bulbil "seeds" in the flower, or by producing healthy cloves for cloning. Most growers choose to plant cloves, which is far easier and faster; however, you can cultivate bulbils by allowing the garlic scapes to reach their full maturity.

Whether or not you plan to grow garlic, learning about the growing process of this fascinating plant will help you dream up creative cooking methods to make the most of garlic through the seasons. Here are a few key terms to help you recognize the different parts of a garlic plant.

BULB. The garlic bulb is the edible root that is also sometimes referred to as a head. The terms are interchangeable, but you will notice that I mostly use the word *bulb* when describing our crop. Each bulb is composed of multiple cloves, covered in many paper layers. They can range in color from purple striped to shades of pink, or even pure white.

CLOVES. The cloves are the individual sections of the bulb. These are what a recipe will typically call for. Each clove develops into a new bulb through asexual reproduction.

SCAPE. The scape is the flowering stalk of a hardneck garlic plant. It grows out of the center of the leaves, creating pigtail-like curls. The scape is entirely edible, with a snappy, asparagus-like texture. It has a mild garlicky flavor and is considered to be the "early" or summer garlic option.

UMBEL. The umbel is the actual flower that is full of tiny miniature bulbs, or bulbils (see below). The umbel develops as the noticeable lump just before the tip of the garlic scape. Although the flower of a garlic plant is not technically a true flower, if allowed to mature, the umbel will open to reveal the bulbils.

BULBIL. These tiny garlic nuggets are contained within the umbel. Each bulbil is genetically identical to the parent plant and will eventually grow into a bulb, but generally it requires at least two growing seasons to be ready to harvest. The main advantage of growing with bulbils is that it produces garlic better acclimated to your specific zone, and it decreases the risk of soilborne diseases.

hardneck garlic

SPATHE

SCAPE

UMBEL

V-KEELED LEAF

STALK

BULB

ROOTS

Growing Garlic through the Seasons

The growing cycle of garlic is slightly different from that of most other edible crops. Typically, plants such as tomatoes, peppers, and potatoes are seeded in spring and harvested in summer or fall. Garlic's life cycle is the opposite—its journey begins in fall.

Growers of garlic can expect to fall in love with the exceptional flavor of homegrown bulbs and feel satisfied knowing they have lovingly cared for their plants from start to finish, from autumn all the way to the following summer. If you're being introduced to the art of growing garlic for the first time, it can be helpful to look at the entire life cycle in steps through the four seasons (the dates or months may differ slightly based on where you live).

Fall

As the calendars roll over to September, we in the Northern Hemisphere naturally brace ourselves for a change in weather. Darkness lingers later in the morning, and there is a crispness in the evening air. Seemingly overnight, the landscape changes dramatically from green to a sea of gold, a telltale sign of autumn. Fall has always been associated with harvest, but when you're growing garlic, the season ends with a new beginning as the next crop is seeded.

Many novice growers have the common misconception that garlic cannot thrive in a cold climate. It might seem almost foolhardy to place sensitive cloves into the earth just before winter, a season that in my region could easily see temperatures plummet to –40°F/–40°C. Trust me, if you have ever felt this or thought it to be true, you are not alone! Many times the first cloves are planted with doubt and trepidation, racing against Mother Nature as snow looms on the horizon. With a few tips and tricks, you will be happily surprised to find just how well garlic thrives, even in some of the harshest

SOWING HOPE

Farming is a profession of hope. We hope that the seeds we place in the soil will germinate and sprouts will reach toward the sky. We hope for better weather in spring, and then we hope for rain in summer. We believe that by taking care of the land we will be rewarded and that we will have the means to continue this lifestyle. And above all else, we have faith that our crops will stand tall.

conditions. Garlic is an ancient crop that time and time again has proven itself to be tough, hearty, and resilient—in a way, it is everything that we often strive to be ourselves.

Planting season at our farm is a whirlwind. The days are full of the sounds of cracking garlic bulbs, their papers flying through the air. Through this organized chaos, we keep one goal determinedly in mind—to plant a hearty crop of garlic.

Over the course of a few weeks, rows upon rows of cloves are seeded. Each clove is placed carefully at the proper depth and covered firmly with soil. The shape of a new field or bed slowly forms as bright stakes are driven into the ground to mark the boundaries. In colder zones (USDA Hardiness Zone 5 and below), this task usually occurs in mid-October, giving the cloves just enough time to set roots before being tucked in for the long winter ahead.

Winter

Winter is meant to be a time of rest. Much like those who cultivate it, garlic requires a dormant period before emerging strong in spring. Where I live, the first snowflakes mark the end of a long growing season, often one that is rife with obstacles to overcome and that leaves farmers exhausted and ready for a change of pace. It is the time to nourish our bodies with wholesome, hearty foods and to take comfort in the coziness of warm homes and sweaters. Winter is a time to reflect on what went wrong this year, to let sore muscles recuperate, and to slowly begin planning for the year ahead. On our farm, the snow covers the ground in an endless white blanket that tucks the garlic in for its long sleep, protecting it from winter's frosty kiss.

In cold climates that don't have reliable snow cover, growers can add a thick layer of straw mulch to protect the cloves. In moderate zones, the cloves usually send up small sprouts before winter sets in. The green shoots stay aboveground but don't grow much, thus providing an adequate dormant period for proper clove development. A light dusting of snow won't harm the shoots; rather, it provides a small amount of insulation and moisture to the plants. Garlic grown in warmer zones, such as southern and coastal California (Zone 9), generally stands tall and grows through the winter season.

While the current year's planting is resting in the ground, you can enjoy this year's harvest. Once properly dried and trimmed, most garlic varieties will last six to eight months on average, often longer, making it a true winter storage crop. Nothing beats the taste of fresh garlic; it's such a treat to have at a time of year when many other locally grown vegetables are unavailable.

Spring

Spring is an exciting time of year on the farm and in the garden. Little by little, the earth comes back to life after a long winter. The change in seasons is welcomed like an old familiar friend. The days slowly become longer, gaining a few minutes of sunlight each day, as evenings extend and allow us to soak up the much-needed vitamin D after months spent mostly in the dark. Spring is bursting with life, from the smallest animals to the new green buds forming on tree branches. There is a renewed freshness in the air as spring brings happy feelings of new beginnings.

Spring weather greatly affects the beginning of the garlic growing season. A cold and drawn-out start can leave growers wondering about what is happening deep beneath the topsoil. You may need to pull straw mulch away from rows to aid in warming the soil.

After the frost gives way and the soil warms, the cloves we planted in fall start to germinate and tiny sprouts stretch upward. Garlic is almost always one of the first crops to pop up in spring. The bright green hues lined up in rows amid the dark soil is a refreshing and reassuring sight. From there the plants' advancement is noticeable as their first leaves form and their stalks shoot toward the sky. In warmer regions, the beginning of spring is marked by new growth in the garlic patch. The small shoots that survived winter welcome the warmth of the sun to restart their journey. The plants develop a healthy green color and begin to stretch upward.

For gardeners, spring is often hectic, a season when everything needs to be done at the same time—except for the garlic, of course. The bulbs are already growing, and you can focus on other crops. Savor that first taste of sunshine on your shoulders while working between the rows. Envision future harvest goals as you plant each tiny seed. Take the time to freshen up the compost pile and begin adding scraps to it again. While you're at it, apply some of that nitrogen-rich compost to your garlic plants as a topdressing; it will give the plants a boost as they emerge and grow aboveground.

One thing to watch for during spring runoff is standing water in your garlic plot. The plants require a fair amount of water, especially during the heat of summer, but they do not like sitting in it. Cloves are prone to rotting if left in water for too long. Dig trenches if necessary to drain excess water off the area.

THE SEASON OF REBIRTH

As spring brings life back to the land, the garden does the same for me. The slumbering soil awakens with new growth, bursting with welcomed activity as the dormant garlic begins to sprout. Each year I look forward to hearing the trilling of a wren and the calling cackle of the red-winged blackbirds. I spend many days traversing sleepy forests looking for deer sheds and listening to the drumming of a ruffed grouse. I am reborn when the snow begins to melt and I can explore for endless hours outside, marveling at the feel of fresh dirt between my toes once again.

Summer

Summer is the most exciting season of garlic's growing cycle. There is a profound feeling of contentment in watching your garden grow, knowing that you are carefully nurturing plants that will feed your family. The days are long but oh, so worth it!

Garlic grows rapidly during the hottest part of the year. In ideal conditions, the summer months see warm temperatures (77°F/25°C and above) that, when combined with the lengthened daylight hours, create prime opportunity for growth. Garlic loves heat, gaining in girth daily by soaking up the sun. You can help your crop along by maintaining a strict weeding regimen to rid your plot of competition for essential nutrients. On average, garlic foliage will reach up to 2 feet high. The overall width of the stalks will also increase and give you a solid estimation of the size of bulbs forming beneath the surface.

SCAPE SEASON

If you are growing hardneck varieties, the flowering part of the plant begins to form after the plant has produced multiple sets of leaves. You'll first notice a small spike coming out of the center of the leaves. As the spike rises, the umbel—a small, rounded portion—will emerge. From there it is only a matter of time, often just a day or two, before the scapes grow into their iconic loops. When we remove the flowerlike portion, the plant's energy is redirected to its roots, so that we cultivate larger and healthier bulbs. The first scapes mark the beginning of a fast-and-furious harvest window.

Many garlic growers spend their summer mornings between the rows of garlic, gathering the curly green stalks—a prized fresh ingredient for gardeners and chefs alike. While there is no defined rule, scapes are best harvested during the early hours when the air is still cool and the plants heavy with dew. Picking then is a calming experience and one to be cherished.

Garlic scape season typically comes to an abrupt halt just two or three weeks after the first scapes are picked. After the last ones have been snapped off, the focus immediately shifts toward the end goal: bulb harvest! The heads gain the majority of their bulk in the coming weeks, the final effort of growth before the leaves begin to die back.

HARVESTTIME

Depending on your region, after 6–10 months of maturing, the garlic is ready to come out of the ground in late summer. In Alberta (USDA Hardiness Zone 3), we aim to begin our harvest near the middle of August; in warmer climates garlic harvest can begin as early as June. The ripeness of the bulbs is demonstrated by the browning of the leaves; it is common practice to harvest after two sets of the bottom leaves have browned. Garlic bulbs require a gentle touch as they are carefully lifted from the soil; gardeners use a shovel or garden fork to loosen the soil around the bulbs until the roots give way.

The final step in the garlic cycle is curing. A drying period is necessary to ensure successful winter storage of the pungent bulb we all love. The weeks tick by and summer fades into fall as the garlic dries. Once the leaves have died back and the bulbs no longer feel damp, they can be removed from the drying racks. The leaves are trimmed to just a small stem, and roots are cut off. A gentle brushing results in beautiful, gleaming garlic bulbs. While the end of the harvest season is a little bittersweet, each bulb brings us one step closer to the start of a new year as we come full circle to the beginning once more—seeding garlic in fall.

WHY FRESH TASTES BETTER

It's often said that homegrown food tastes best, and garlic is no exception. The powerful taste of a bulb fresh out of the garden will leave you so excited that you're likely to vow never to buy garlic at the store again. Fortunately, you don't have to grow vast quantities of bulbs to appreciate the superiority of fresh garlic. Fresh garlic is known for its extremely pungent cloves, in part because it has not been sitting long enough for the flavors to slowly deteriorate; store-bought garlic has. Garlic grown in sulfur-rich soil will also be more pungent.

Thirty-three sulfur compounds naturally occur in garlic, the most relevant being allicin, which gives garlic its spicy essence. Because of this, garlic has a high soil sulfur requirement. Garlic plants absorb sulfur through their roots; the amount of sulfur in the garden soil directly correlates to how hot the cloves taste. Some experts suspect that low sulfur levels contribute to higher occurrences of rotting bulbs, although that has not been proven yet. If your soil has a sulfur deficiency, many natural options can increase the levels. Manure, for example, can contribute sufficient sulfur—though in a slow-release form. Compost with broken-down organic matter may contribute to soil sulfur, and organic sulfur fertilizers are available as well. However, even though we all crave hot-flavored garlic, there is such a thing as too much sulfur. Be cautious when using commercial sulfur amendments, and follow the instructions on the package.

Choosing Seed Garlic

The term *seed garlic* can sometimes be confusing, as technically any bulb can be replanted, but seed garlic bulbs are those deemed most suitable for replanting and growing next year's crop. For most growers, that means the largest unblemished bulbs. Seed garlic should not be treated with any chemicals, so if you are purchasing seed garlic instead of using your own, do your due diligence and confirm with your seed source whether or not their bulbs are treated before planting any seed bulbs.

Garlic reproduces through asexual propagation, meaning it does not require pollination. A garlic clove, or seed, is a genetic copy of the parent plant. The new bulbs are clones of the ones they came from—a fact that reinforces the importance of using high-quality garlic seed when planting your crop.

Determine how much to plant based on your garden plot size, how many bulbs you think you might eat throughout winter, and how big a crop you may want to grow next year. Choose to overplant, opting for too much instead of too little, to combat the losses often associated with winterkill, subpar growing conditions (flooding, hail), and pests. Any excess bulbs come fall can become a beautiful gift to family and friends, or can be utilized as seed for the following year's crop.

It's helpful to work through the math to know just how many seed bulbs you will need. For example, assuming you space the cloves 6 inches apart, a 20-foot row would yield 40 bulbs of garlic. 'Red Russian' bulbs average four to six cloves, so if each seed bulb were to offer five planting cloves, you would require eight seed bulbs for the 20-foot row.

Softneck or Hardneck?

The first step in choosing seed garlic is to decide whether to grow softneck or hardneck garlic. Pay close attention to the limitations within your growing zone, as some varieties may not be suited to your region.

HARDNECK. Hardneck garlic bulbs produce a garlic scape, the flowering stalk of the plant, and are generally hardier than their softneck cousins. For colder climates (USDA Hardiness Zone 5 and below), choose a hardneck garlic that will withstand the extended winter periods. I have great luck growing the varieties 'Red Russian', 'Music', and 'Tibetan', which have proven to be quite hardy in our growing zone in Alberta.

SOFTNECK. Known for their extended storage life, softneck garlic bulbs are an excellent choice for kitchen gardens in warmer regions. Softneck varieties are heat-tolerant and are best suited for USDA Hardiness Zone 6 and above.

Where to Source Seed Garlic

If possible, try to source your garlic seed as locally as you can. Bulbs grown in your region will already be acclimated to your weather conditions. Shop at local farmers' markets or buy directly from garlic growers. If you are unable to find a local source, look to trusted seed companies for seed bulbs, or check out a nearby garden center or greenhouse.

Set yourself and your future crop up for success by using only high-quality seed. If you are able to choose individual bulbs from a local supplier, look for ones that feel firm and are free of bruising. Also choose the biggest bulbs you can; bigger bulbs with bigger cloves will grow bigger plants.

Do not plant garlic from the grocery store. You cannot be sure of its origins, how it was grown, or how fresh it is. Chances are a bulb from the grocery store has been sprayed with preservatives to prevent it from sprouting and it will not grow well in your garden.

Propagating Garlic Using Bulbils

Planting using bulbils is a way to exponentially increase your crop size.
By allowing the garlic scapes to fully mature, you will be able to use the
bulbils as seed. (See page 196 for harvest information.) However, bulbils
require at least two and up to four years to develop into proper bulbs.
The process is lengthy, which is why most growers choose to plant cloves.

To propagate using bulbils, in fall plant the tiny garlic pieces 1 inch deep and
2 to 3 inches apart. Cover with soil and add a layer of mulch to protect them
during winter. Allow them to sprout and grow foliage in spring and summer.
After the first year of growing, most bulbils will develop a single, round clove.
Carefully remove the clove from the soil using a fork or shovel, and hang it
to dry, much as you would a regular bulb. Once the foliage has dried suffi-
ciently, trim the roots and stalk. Plant the round clove in fall to grow again for
another year. Follow good crop-rotation practices and rotate the garlic plot
to a new location for the next growing season to minimize pest and disease
risks (see page 182). Bulbils can also be planted in spring, provided they are
stored properly through winter.

Timing Your Planting

Hardneck garlic needs a period of cold-temperature dormancy (called vernalization) for it to grow properly. Without enough of a cold period, hardneck garlic can form misshapen bulbs that lack clove development, often resulting in just one giant clove or onion-type bulb. The dormancy period varies by variety, but on average most hardneck garlics require at least eight weeks of temperatures below 40°F (5°C). Vernalization (from the Latin *vernus*, meaning "of spring") also triggers the garlic to sprout when the weather warms.

Softneck garlic does not require a dormancy period and therefore can be planted in both spring and fall.

Planting in Fall

In regions that have cold winters (averaging below −4°F/−20°C), garlic is planted in fall. Ideally the cloves should be planted at least two weeks before the first hard frost, so that it can set roots before going dormant. There is a bit of wiggle room, though, and it is always better to plant late than early. If temperatures are still warm when you plant garlic, the cloves may send up shoots, which are frost sensitive. The shoots, if allowed to grow before winter, will most likely succumb to winter's icy clutches, resulting in winterkill. Here in Alberta (USDA Hardiness Zone 3), we aim to plant our garlic by the middle of October.

Planting in a milder climate has a few key differences. Cloves can be planted up to six weeks prior to the first frost date, giving them ample time to set roots and begin to sprout. Since the frost date is quite a bit later, this means cloves can be planted as early as October or as late as December. The traditional recommendation was to plant garlic on the shortest day of the year and harvest it on the longest day. Look to the frost dates of your specific zone to determine when your garlic should be planted. Don't be alarmed if you see little shoots of green popping up before winter sets in. The garlic sprouts may even stay green throughout winter; however, you won't notice any significant growth until spring. While the presence of garlic sprouts can be a concern in cold regions, the tiny sprouts will overwinter just fine in milder climates. Consider mulching your garlic to further protect it in case of a cold snap and to help suppress weeds.

Planting in Spring

The general recommendation is that most garlic varieties, especially hardneck varieties, be planted in fall. That said, planting in spring can still yield rows of bulbs. If you miss the fall window, use the following advice to grow a spring-planted crop.

- Be sure to properly store seed garlic through winter to ensure a healthy crop (see page 210).

- Plant garlic cloves as soon as the earth can be worked in spring. Or, if your area experiences a period of warm weather during winter (to the point where the ground is soft), you can sneak out to the garden and plant your garlic then.

- Feed plants with generous amounts of fertilizer once they emerge, and keep the rows free of weeds to ensure the bulbs receive the highest amount of nutrients possible, since they are already making up for lost days.

- Be aware that planting spring garlic in cool growing zones (USDA Hardiness Zone 5 and below) may result in smaller bulbs or rounds (single-clove bulbs).

- The success of a spring garlic crop is wholly dependent on the zone you grow in. Reach out to fellow growers within your area for help and advice.

Choosing the Best Site
for Growing Garlic

Successful gardening is all about putting the right plant in the right spot, and garlic is no exception. Thankfully, garlic has many of the same needs as other crops in the vegetable garden, including:

LOOSE, WELL-DRAINING SOIL. Heavy soil that retains water can lead to rotting. Add compost, broken-down leaves, or other organic matter to improve the tilth of your soil. (Tilth is the quality of the physical condition of soil, making it more or less suitable for growing.) Avoid planting in low spots that collect water.

FULL SUN. Choose a location that receives at least 6 hours (8 to 10 hours preferred) of sun each day. If possible, plant in north-to-south rows for optimal sun exposure.

REGULAR MOISTURE. If your region does not receive regular rainfall in summer, be sure to locate your garlic beds in a spot with easy access of irrigation. Garlic needs roughly an inch of water per week during the growing season.

Select Sites That Capture Snow
A thick layer of snow helps insulate and protect garlic when winter temperatures reach their coldest, reducing the chances of winterkill. If you live in a windy landscape where snow blows away, consider using snow fences to trap snow over your garlic beds, or plant in a spot where snow naturally accumulates.

WHEN WINTER COMES EARLY

A few years ago, winter struck as we were attempting to seed our garlic crop in mid- to late October. It was a challenging year from start to finish, made worse by the fact that our seeding equipment broke down and we were facing the colossal task of planting 20,000 cloves by hand! Thankfully, my whole family came to my aid to get the cloves in the ground. That fall, we were planting garlic directly into snow. The earth underneath wasn't frozen yet, so we were still able to work the soil. There was a huge celebration all around once shoots became visible in spring.

Consider Crop Rotation

To grow a healthy crop of garlic that is free of fungus or garlic rust, avoid planting garlic in areas where alliums (garlic, onions, leeks) or other root vegetables have recently been grown. In the gardening world, this is called crop rotation. To minimize pest and disease issues, growers rotate their crops from one bed to the next, so that a crop is grown in a particular bed only every three to five years.

You can use cover crops in your own crop rotation to help maintain healthy soil beds. Cover crops improve soil tilth and structure and reduce soil compaction. They are also known as "green manures" that fix (capture) nitrogen and provide many added nutrients when turned into the soil. Flowering cover crops have the benefit of attracting pollinators to your garden.

There are many options available, but popular choices among growers include:

• Red clover

• Annual ryegrass

• Buckwheat

• Alfalfa

On our farm, we follow a five-year rotation plan. In the off years when we are not planting garlic in a particular field, we grow alfalfa as a cover crop. It protects against topsoil erosion, adds organic matter to the soil, and provides a natural food source for many wild animals. We also sell some of the alfalfa as cut hay.

Companion Planting with Garlic

When you are choosing a site for growing your garlic, you might consider which crops make good companions. Companion planting is based on the idea that certain crops grow better with some plants than they do with others. While much of the information about companion planting is anecdotal, many gardeners find the practice effective.

Plant garlic close to companion plants such as:

- **FRUIT TREES.** The strong odor of garlic repels pests such as fruit tree borer and mites. It is also suggested that the tree may be made more resistant to fungus by absorbing the sulfur produced by garlic.

- **CARROTS.** Garlic, as well as onion, repels carrot root flies.

- **TOMATOES.** Garlic helps to keep away aphids, caterpillars, and slugs.

- **ROSES.** The pungent smell of sulfur repels aphids from roses.

- **MINT.** The strong aroma of this perennial herb helps deter onion maggots that may infest garlic bulbs. It is also thought to improve the flavor of garlic. Be mindful that mint does spread rapidly. Consider planting it in pots near your garlic as opposed to planting it in the ground.

Avoid planting garlic near plants such as:

- **BEANS AND PEAS.** Garlic is believed to stunt the growth of vegetables in the legume family.

- **ONIONS.** Planting garlic close to onions may encourage the development of onion maggots and other allium pests.

Garlic *and* Mint Pest Repellent

The pungent smell of garlic is often more than enough to deter garden pests. In fact, it is the allicin and sulfur found within the cloves that make it a useful pest repellent. You can prepare a spray incorporating garlic and mint to repel aphids, spider mites, and ants. Take care to spray on the underside of plants during the evening hours or on cloudy days to avoid sunburnt leaves.

1 garlic bulb

1 cup mint leaves

6 cups water

1 tablespoon castile soap or natural dish soap

1 tablespoon cayenne pepper (optional)

1   Finely chop the garlic and let it stand for 10 minutes to allow the allicin levels to reach their maximum. Finely chop the mint leaves.

2   Place the garlic, mint, and water in a large pot. Bring to a boil and let simmer for 15 minutes. Set aside to cool.

3   Strain the cooled mixture, discarding the solids, and then add the soap. Stir in the cayenne pepper, if using. Let stand overnight. Keep in the refrigerator for up to 1 week.

Prepare the Soil for Planting

Prepare the beds by loosening the soil with a broadfork or rototiller. If need be, amend the soil with a rich compost, but avoid adding too much nitrogen in fall. Garlic cloves need phosphorus to develop roots, so focus on a fertilizer blend that is high in that mineral. If the soil is dry, water the bed deeply enough so that moisture is available at the cloves' planting depth.

If you are curious about your soil's fertility, you can perform a soil test. Soil tests can be quite helpful in assessing the state of your garden plot. A simple, inexpensive at-home test kit (found at most garden centers) will help you determine the pH as well as the levels of basic nutrients. In many areas of the US, people can have more detailed soil tests performed and analyzed by a local agricultural station or Cooperative Extension Service.

Planting Garlic

Each garlic clove is a seed, so you will need to crack the bulbs open and separate the cloves. Once the heads have been broken apart, be careful not to peel the cloves. The tough papery husks prevent pests, such as wireworms, or fungal diseases from gaining access to the cloves once they are in the ground.

For easy cracking, turn the bulb upside down in your hand and, with a firm grip, smash the stem downward on a hard surface. This pushes the stem and root bundle upward, freeing the cloves.

Determining Clove Depth and Spacing

Plant the cloves "nose up," with the pointy tip facing upward. This will help produce straight stems on your future bulbs. Some people find it easier to make a furrow—a narrow trench in the soil—and gently drop the cloves down the line. Alternatively, you can gently dig a hole to place each individual clove.

Place the cloves 4 to 6 inches apart and approximately 2 to 3 inches deep. Rows should be spaced 12 inches apart. If your garden bed is small, or if you choose to plant in a raised bed, you can stagger the cloves in square blocks, maintaining at least 4 inches between the cloves.

Once the cloves are placed in their rows or individual planting holes, cover them with soil and gently pack the earth to tuck them in for the long winter ahead.

Mulching for Insulation

It's a good idea to mulch your garlic beds after planting, to insulate the cloves in winter as well as protect them during periods of temperature fluctuation—such as in spring, when a week or two of warm weather may be followed by a deep freeze. If the soil begins to warm up, the uninsulated cloves may sprout and then be killed by the sudden freeze.

At planting time, apply a 2- to 3-inch-thick layer of mulch. Wheat or barley straw make excellent mulches, but be cautious when using hemp or flaxseed straw as these tend to form a mat too tough for shoots to pass through. There are many other options for mulching that you may choose from, including leaves and grass clippings, alfalfa hay, and compost. I prefer to use wheat straw mulch in my own garden because it is readily available on our farm.

Although there is no such thing as too much mulch when it comes to protecting your cloves, be aware that excessively thick layers can attract rodents looking for a winter home, and their digging could disturb roots. Thick mulching may also result in late germination. For that reason, when the weather warms in spring, rake the mulch away to help warm the soil and allow the tender shoots to poke through. Once the cloves have sprouted, rake the mulch back onto the beds to suppress weeds and help maintain soil moisture levels. At the end of the season, after the bulbs have been harvested, compost the straw or dig it into the soil to break down and improve the tilth.

Growing in Raised Beds

Raised beds are convenient, comfortable, and popular in backyard gardens. Many gardeners wonder whether garlic can be successfully grown in them. The answer is yes, but with caution. Garlic grown in regions subject to extreme winter conditions will almost always do better when sown directly into the ground. But with a little extra care, garlic can thrive in raised beds nearly anywhere.

With raised beds, special attention needs to be given to insulation to avoid the effects of temperature fluctuations, which are felt more acutely in beds above the native soil. Heavily mulch the beds and, if possible, provide insulation on the sides as well. Plant the cloves in the center, away from the bed edges, for added protection. During the hot summer months, you may need to water more frequently.

Some northern growers have been able to grow garlic in planters (at least 12 inches deep) stored in a cold room (in temperatures less than 40°F/5°C) throughout winter. Once the weather warms in spring, the pot or planter can be moved outdoors. To prevent shock from the change in conditions, expose the planter to outdoor elements gradually before repositioning it to a sunny location for summer. Shallow planters dry out quickly, and you may need to water more frequently.

Care during the Growing Season

Relatively speaking, garlic is a low-maintenance crop. Unlike other crops, such as tomatoes, that need to be pruned regularly, garlic requires very little assistance to thrive. When grown under the right conditions, impressive yields of big, beautiful bulbs are easily managed. There are, of course, a few key points to keep in mind to help maintain the health of your crop.

Fertilizing Your Garlic

Garlic is a heavy feeder: It requires a fair amount of nitrogen, potassium, and phosphorus throughout the growing season to yield healthy bulbs. Apply a small amount of balanced organic fertilizer (one with equal percentages of nitrogen, phosphorus, and potassium) at the beginning of the season, according to the manufacturer's guidelines. You can also choose to topdress by applying a generous helping of compost on the soil surface around plants. Fertilizer can be applied again after the plants set true leaves, but be sure to stop applications by the time scapes begin to form. Always water deeply after applying fertilizer—both to make the nutrients more accessible to the plants' roots and to mitigate potential stress caused by the influx of nutrients.

There is, of course, a balance between fertilizing enough to promote growth and overfeeding. Too much fertilizer can burn the plants (evidenced by yellowing or browning tips) or stimulate excessive foliage growth, causing the plants to become top-heavy. Although essential nutrients are important, using dependable seed garlic to begin with will be the most helpful in obtaining big bulbs.

Stirrup hoe

Keeping Up with Weeds

One of the best things you can do for your garlic patch is to keep it weed-free. As soon as tiny sprouts are visible in spring, spend a little time each week working down the rows or garden patch to manage the weeds. Staying on top of the weeds can be overwhelming at times, but your future self will thank you for pulling them when they are young; it is much easier to pull small roots! With less competition, garlic plants will have access to all of the soil nutrients and will hopefully develop into large bulbs come fall.

Believe it or not, I actually enjoy the subtle art of weeding. Performing monotonous tasks with my hands allows my mind to wander, to solve all of life's toughest problems and to form plans for the future. This kind of work is hugely beneficial to my mental health, not to mention the many grounding benefits of physically working with soil.

My weeding tool of choice is a stirrup hoe. It allows you to work around the plants and cuts off weeds at the ground. Best of all, it is easy on your back to use, and you need not spend all day bent over or on your knees.

Ensuring the Right Amount of Water

Garlic requires regular watering throughout the growing season, but not to the point where the soil is oversaturated. Aim to give plants roughly 1 inch of water per week.

Monitor the level of moisture in your soil by asking yourself these questions:

- Does the topsoil look dry?

- Can you feel moisture if you stick a finger into the soil?

- Is there standing water?

Generally speaking, once the top inch of soil has dried, it is time to water. Allow the water to fully soak into the rows before watering again. Garlic will rot if its roots are left in standing water, so be careful not to apply too much water (you should not see pools collecting). Mulching the garlic bed will also help preserve moisture in the soil.

When bulb harvesttime nears, taper off the irrigation. Stop watering roughly two weeks prior to harvest to aid in the drying and curing of the bulbs. The dry conditions stimulate the plants to shift into their final stages of growth, causing their energy to reach the bulbs instead of the foliage, which is indicated by the bottom leaves' browning.

Much like the other vegetables grown in your garden, garlic benefits from the use of a natural water source. If you are able, irrigate your beds with collected rainfall. Municipal tap water is better than nothing, but it does contain minerals, occasionally along with chlorine, fluoride, and other chemicals to make it safe for human consumption, which can be toxic to plants over time.

WATERFRONT REAL ESTATE

When it comes to selecting a site for one of our garlic fields, water is always at the forefront of my mind. Having easy access to water is essential to growing garlic during harsh drought conditions. We choose to irrigate by drawing from a natural source, one of our fish ponds. Our garlic plots all sit within reach of one of these ponds, making the most idyllic settings I could ever imagine growing in.

5

picking and preserving garlic

The garlic harvest is a celebration in itself! The triumphant yields of curled garlic scapes and flavorful bulbs point to all the hard work you put into managing a healthy crop. Take time to savor the bounty of your efforts as you honor your accomplishments in the garden. Garlic is a unique crop to grow because of its two distinct harvests. By learning how to properly harvest both the garlic scapes and bulbs, you will find new ways to take pleasure in their different flavors and culinary uses. Have fun with it and celebrate the completion of a year of garlic.

Garlic Scape Season

Garlic scape season is a highly anticipated time of year for growers of hardneck varieties. The curly stalks mark the beginning of the garlic harvest, each one a tasty preview of what is yet to come. In my region (USDA Hardiness Zone 3), the first scapes emerge by the beginning of July, although gardeners may see them as early as May in warmer climates. Garlic scapes are arguably the wackiest vegetable out there and can best be described as a green-tasting garlic. While their flavor is still intense, they tend not to be quite as hot as a fresh garlic bulb. The difference is similar to that of scallions compared to an onion bulb.

Harvesting the hardneck garlic scapes is not necessary, but it is recommended. Once the scapes are removed, the plant's energy is redirected from developing seeds to developing the roots and bulb. A garlic bulb will still form whether scapes are picked or left on, but there will be a noticeable difference in bulb size. Opt to remove the garlic scape if growing large heads of garlic is your goal.

The aroma that accompanies scape harvests is second to none. A mouth-watering mix of garlic and heavy dew floats through the air as you snap the scapes off one by one. It is a pleasurable task to walk up and down the rows and gather scapes by hand, filling harvest bins or baskets. Once harvested, garlic scapes have an astonishingly long shelf life, often lasting well into the summer months or fall if stored properly. To me, garlic scapes taste like summer, and they mellow quite nicely as they are cooked. They can be enjoyed a number of different ways, from side dishes to bold pesto (see pages 62 to 82 for recipes).

How and When to Harvest Garlic Scapes

Harvesting garlic scapes is very easy. Simply snap the scape off near its base (at the junction of the top leaves) using your thumb and index finger. Alternatively, you can cut them off with garden shears. The best time to pick garlic scapes is in the early morning. Aim to harvest before the heat of the day sets in to prevent them from wilting.

Many gardeners prefer to harvest young garlic scapes for their tender stalks. The supple stems have a snappy texture, similar to asparagus. While there is no perfect time, a general rule of thumb is to allow the garlic scapes to form one full curl, with the umbel crossing over the stalk.

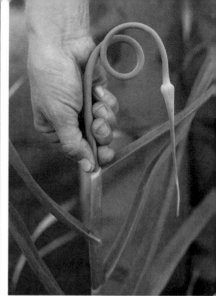

Have fun while you harvest! The easiest way to carry the scapes (and keep your hands free to continue picking) is to create "scape bracelets." Let the scapes curl around your wrists and keep adding them until you run out of room.

If left too long, the scapes become woody and quite fibrous, making eating them a little less appealing. But you can still utilize the tougher scapes: Dehydrate them to grind into garlic scape powder and seasonings (see page 199) or set them aside to be added to flavorful simmering broths. The long stems can be a playful addition to a bouquet of garden blooms (see page 130). Allowing the scapes to mature also brings forth the exciting opportunity to cultivate the bulbils, the mini garlic cloves found within the umbel.

Harvesting Garlic Bulbils

Within the umbel, or flower, of the garlic scape are the small garlic bulbils. Each bulbil is a genetic copy of the parent plant that does not require pollination. The bulbils are an interesting feature of hardneck garlic, since they can either be eaten or planted. Using garlic bulbils is an efficient way to increase your crop size. Instead of the usual six cloves that a garlic bulb will produce, there are sometimes hundreds of bulbils within one garlic scape!

There are benefits to harvesting garlic bulbils.

• You get a large quantity of seed from just one bulbil.

• Less space is required to grow bulbils (for the first year).

• The likelihood of soil diseases in your seed is decreased as the bulbils never actually touch the earth until they are planted.

And there are disadvantages.

• It takes a minimum of two years to harvest a garlic bulb grown from a bulbil, and sometimes up to four years depending on the variety.

• Growing with bulbils requires the same amount of work on the back end— weeding, watering, harvesting, drying, storing—as growing with garlic bulbs.

To harvest the bulbils, allow the garlic scapes to fully mature, so that the umbel opens. Snap or cut the scapes off the plants at their junction with the top set of leaves. Let them dry in a safe location, out of direct sunlight, until the bulbils are firm. Should you decide to use the bulbils as seed, see page 178 for planting instructions.

Note that the cluster of bulbils is edible. It can be roasted whole, similar to a bulb, and is a striking addition to a charcuterie spread (see page 82 for a recipe). You can also gently pry the bulbils apart and mince to sauté directly in a pan.

Garlic Scape Storage Tips

Once the garlic scapes have been harvested, follow these tricks to maximize their storage life. You will be amazed at how long the stems stay fresh.

- Rinse the garlic scapes in cold water to keep them crisp.

- Trim the ends of the stems and place in a jar or glass of cool water (as you would treat flowers in a vase). Store in the fridge, changing the water and trimming the bottom of the stems every few days.

- If need be, remove the upper portion of the scape (including the umbel and tip) and set aside to use in pesto. Store the lower portions of the scapes in a lidded container with a damp piece of paper towel.

- Freeze garlic scapes to last throughout winter.

Preserving Garlic Scapes

The scape season is plentiful but very quick—if you blink, you might miss it! Preserving your scapes by freezing or dehydrating them allows you to enjoy this taste of summer at a more leisurely pace.

How to Dehydrate Garlic Scapes

Dehydrating garlic scapes is a great way to make the most of your bounty. Break the scapes into small pieces or run them through a food processor before dehydrating (this makes them easier to grind later). Dry scapes in a food dehydrator at 130°F (55°C) for 10 hours, or until completely dry. Once cooled, place the dry garlic scapes in a spice grinder or clean coffee grinder. Pulse until the desired texture is reached. Sift the powder through a fine-mesh strainer to catch any large pieces. Return the large pieces to the grinder or set aside to be used as a coarse grind.

You can adjust the coarseness of the grind for different uses. For soups, I like to use bigger chunks that soften as they cook, but I prefer a fine powder to sprinkle over baked potatoes. Find what works best for you.

How to Freeze Garlic Scapes

Garlic scapes freeze well with minimal prep, and they can be stored for up to six months. Simply cut the scapes into very fine pieces, then pack in a freezer bag, removing as much air as possible.

You can also use a food processor to make garlic scape cubes. Place the scapes in a food processor and pulse until finely minced. Form into 1-inch cubes. Arrange the cubes on a baking sheet lined with parchment paper and place in the freezer to set. Alternatively, pack the pulsed scapes into an ice cube tray. Once frozen solid, remove the cubes from the baking sheet or ice cube tray and store in a freezer bag.

HEIRLOOM GARDENING

In my toolshed, I have my great-grandmother's potato fork, which is quite useful in digging roots of all kinds, garlic included! Family and traditions are at the heart of my farm business, in tiny details that make me so proud of where I come from. Being able to repurpose something that has been used for four generations is a way to honor my family's history, and to learn to appreciate doing things the old way.

Garlic Bulb Harvest

First-time growers often wonder how to know when their garlic is ready to be harvested. If you collect the bulbs too early, you might miss the final growth spurt, but if you wait too long, the cloves can grow out of the paper wrappers, causing the bulbs to split and reducing storage time. If left even longer, the bulbs may rot in the ground. Although recognizing the ideal harvesttime can seem a bit daunting at first, there are a few telltale signs that will help you decide when to begin collecting your coveted crop.

- You can expect to harvest hardneck garlic bulbs roughly one month after the scapes have been picked (typically the middle of August where I live).

- Look for at least two sets of bottom leaves to begin turning brown and dying back. This is a sign that the energy is no longer being utilized by the leaves and is being sent into the bulb.

- Dig down into the soil, without upsetting the bulb or roots, and visually assess the bulb. If you can see proper clove development and a healthy-size bulb, it is ready to be picked.

If left in the ground too long, the cloves of the garlic bulb will grow through their protective paper wrappers, resulting in spoilage and fast deterioration. To avoid this, try to harvest while the stems are still upright, with only a few brown leaves.

Harvesting Methods

Be mindful not to pull the plant by its leaves or stem. The roots anchoring the bulbs in the soil are astonishingly strong, and you will more than likely end up pulling the stems right out of the bulbs. If this does happen, use a shovel to carefully uncover the broken bulb. Set any damaged bulbs aside to be used right away. Without the proper paper coverings, the bulb will not store well.

USING A SHOVEL

The simplest harvesting method is to use a fork or shovel to carefully release and lift the bulbs from the ground. Place the fork or shovel a little bit away from the row and gently rock it back and forth to loosen the soil around the garlic roots. With your hand, tenderly pull on the plant to free it from the soil. This might be the most labor-intensive way to harvest the bulbs, but it is also the most cost-effective since the only tool you need is a shovel. It is also the easiest way to dig garlic in tight spaces or small gardens.

UNDERCUT BAR METHOD

If your garlic crop is quite plentiful (and your garden space allows), you might consider using an undercut bar to aid in the release of the roots. Begin by digging a shallow trench across the end of a row, slightly deeper than the bulbs. A large horizontal steel bar is placed in the trench and then pulled by a garden tractor down the length of the row. Once the row has been cut, follow along behind the tractor and gather the bulbs from the soil. The bar makes the bulbs easy to lift out of the soil without risking damage to them. Group the garlic bulbs to create bundles for hanging, and brush off any excess dirt by hand. This method can be quite efficient in harvesting large crop sizes. Ask a few friends to come out to help and make the task at hand more enjoyable.

HARVESTING ABUNDANCE

Our harvest days begin shortly after dawn, before the heat of the day takes over. As the distinct rows begin to disappear, the field that should stand empty is often full of helping hands. Family and friends offer their time to gather bundles. My partner, Paul, arranges days off from work to hang garlic and to just be there as an emotional support to me throughout a hectic and stressful time. More than once neighbors have shown up to help lighten the load, fitting in a visit as we work side by side. We feel camaraderie through a common goal, and laughter can be heard over the hum of the tractor as our community surrounds us.

I will be forever grateful for these people. Many times, nonmaterial things are worth exponentially more than anything in a bank account. I hope to be known someday for having given greatly, and for being rich in the people I chose to surround myself with. On harvest days, I definitely feel rich.

Once the bulbs have all been harvested, they are brushed by hand to remove as much excess dirt as possible. It is essential to get rid of as much dirt as we can, to eliminate any unnecessary weight that could put strain on the wires while the bulbs hang. We then give the bundles a twist to tighten the ties. This allows us to become better acquainted with our crop and inspect for any damaged bulbs that may spoil during the drying stage. The bundles are then loaded into a trailer and transported back to the shed to be hung on the wall.

Hanging and Curing Garlic

Garlic bulbs need to cure after being harvested so the flavors can intensify; the drying process sets the bulbs up for optimal storage as well. When garlic comes out of the ground, it is actually quite soft and sensitive to the touch and can bruise as easily as a peach. The bulbs need to be handled with care as they are gathered and left to cure. There is also the added benefit of a great feeling of accomplishment in seeing all of your hard work on display.

Bundles of garlic should hang for an average of four weeks. Take the humidity into account when assessing how long to let the bulbs dry. In dry years, our drying time stays at a minimum—about three weeks. In wet years, our garlic crop may take more than five weeks to dry fully. Don't rush this process! Let the leaves dry completely, their colors changing from green to brown. Each leaf on the stalk forms a layer in the papery wrappers around the cloves. As the foliage dies back, the papers dry and seal tightly around the bulb. This maximizes storage life and keeps fungal diseases at bay. You can also judge the progress of the bulbs by feeling them to assess whether they are still damp. Be careful not to squeeze too hard or you may end up bruising a bulb that isn't cured yet.

Garlic-Drying Essentials

The drying process is very important in the management of a successful garlic crop. As you plant your first cloves, think ahead about where you will hang your garlic so that you're ready when the bulbs come out of the ground. There are countless ways to hang garlic; choose something that works well in the space you have. It doesn't have to be expensive or elaborate, just so long as it is strong enough to withstand the weight of your crop. Use materials you have at your disposal; find something you already own to repurpose into a unique garlic-drying system. Choose a well-protected spot for your garlic to dry. Look for a place that includes:

ADEQUATE AIRFLOW. Having proper ventilation around the bulbs is key to successful curing. You may want to consider setting up a fan to circulate air around the hanging bulbs to aid with drying.

NO DIRECT SUNLIGHT. It is fine to expose the bulbs to a bit of sunshine while you're harvesting and gathering them, but don't let them dry in full sun. The heat can quickly deteriorate the quality and flavor of the bulbs, almost cooking them, and may lead to poor winter storage.

SAFETY FROM PESTS. While garlic naturally deters most critters, some animals may become curious or accidentally knock over a drying rack. Some nesting birds, such as sparrows, like to build a cozy home in the garlic leaves.

PROTECTION FROM FREEZING TEMPERATURES. Be mindful of frosts and their potential reach if your bulbs are curing in an uninsulated building. Sometimes covering them with a tarp (on cold nights) can be enough protection. But if nighttime temperatures frequently dip below the freezing mark, consider bringing the bulbs into a warmer building.

PROTECTION FROM MOISTURE AND HUMIDITY. Keep bulbs out of reach of any water. Your storage space should be dry.

Garlic bulbs can be hung to dry with bulbs facing up or down, depending on what fits best with your drying system; the bulb direction doesn't matter. No matter how they're arranged, just make sure there is enough room for air to flow between them.

Closet organizer converted into drying rack with bulbs hanging on it

Here are a few examples of innovative homemade drying systems to consider.

- Convert an old closet organizer into a drying rack using chicken wire. Remove the drawers and attach chicken wire to the top of the frame using zip ties. Hang bulbs upside down through the holes.

- Find a sturdy ladder. Tie a piece of twine (or heavy wire) to the steps on each side, creating a line between the A-frame. Hang garlic in bundles along the lines.

- If you don't have the space or materials to hang the bulbs, you can dry them flat with a little extra attentiveness. Spread the bulbs out on newspaper and rotate them each day to ensure there are no damp spots. This can easily be accomplished on a table set up in a dry basement.

OUR GARLIC WALL

The Garlic Wall at our farm stands roughly 20 feet high and is over 100 feet long. The wall tells the story of our season: the long days tending to the field, the amount of rain we received, and ultimately the success of our year. Good or bad, it all goes on display up on the wall. I find it incredibly humbling to see the fruits of my labor all laid out on the line like that. It is a functional drying system that has also become one of my favorite parts of the garlic harvest because of how stunning it is!

The wall developed over time. As my crop size increased, there was a greater need for a large-scale drying rack. Thankfully, my dad's machine shed doubles as the perfect place to hang garlic. It is one of the few structures big enough to house the entire crop. The building is also sheltered from the elements and keeps our bulbs out of direct sunlight. It was built open on both ends so we could drive equipment through—this creates a natural wind tunnel, giving the garlic bulbs more than enough airflow to dry. Passive drying methods like this cut down on input costs and contribute to a more sustainable system. We still have the option of adding fans to help circulate the air; however, the wind tunnel has proven to be more than sufficient.

The garlic is hung on high-tensile wires strung up between the massive studs. The wires are reinforced at each board, while inline tighteners keep them taut. Each bundle straddles the line securely so that the garlic bulbs cannot drop as they hang. By the end of August, the wall is transformed into one made entirely of garlic.

For roughly four weeks, a heavenly scent of the fresh cloves greets you as you walk into the machine shed. You will likely also find the garlic drying with the combine parked nearby, a visual demonstration of generations working together. It is the perfect blending of my worlds: the old with the new, big and small all at once.

With each season, as the wall makes frequent appearances in my social media channels, it becomes more well known and beloved. The uniqueness of our drying system attracts many visitors and farm tour guests, all of whom stand in awe as they take in the scale of thousands of bulbs drying en masse. The overall effect is strikingly beautiful. It has become an iconic symbol of the Fifth Gen brand, a solid wall of pure garlic bliss!

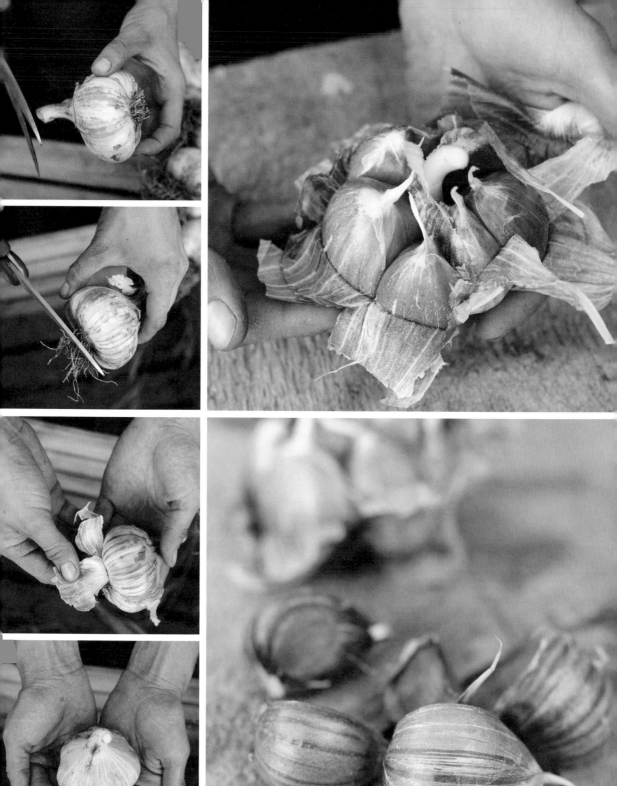

Trimming and Cleaning

Once the leaves have completely dried, trim the stem so that 2 to 3 inches of the neck remains intact. Brush any remaining dirt from the roots using your hands or a stiff-bristled brush. Then trim the roots as close to the bulb as possible. The next step is to gently clean the bulbs, removing any dirt or torn papers—but be careful not to remove too many of the protective paper layers. You can simply rub the bulbs clean with your hands or a paper towel.

After the bulbs have been cleaned, sort them according to size. Keep the smaller bulbs for the kitchen, and set aside the largest bulbs as seed for next year's crop. When choosing which bulbs to use as seed garlic, look for the best-quality bulbs your crop has to offer—the biggest and most uniform. Generally speaking, what you plant is what you get. Commit to using a portion of your cured crop to further your garlic-growing experience in a sustainable way. You can, of course, also choose to purchase seed garlic and save your largest bulbs for roasting (see page 55).

SIZE MATTERS

For my business, my goal is to grow jumbo seed bulbs, big roasters, and easy peelers for our customers. In terms of seed garlic, that means go big or go home! If you are looking for higher quantities and size is not your priority, you can choose to plant smaller cloves. Smaller seed bulbs often sell for less than larger bulbs, making them more cost-effective, and they can be a great way to increase your harvest at less cost. During my first year of growing garlic, I just wanted as many bulbs as possible, so every single clove was planted. Those first bulbs were some of the smallest ones I have ever grown but were still filled with incredible flavor.

Storing Garlic

When it comes to assessing the longevity of your garlic bulbs, pay close attention to storage timelines for specific varieties. On average, most hard-neck bulbs will keep for 4 to 6 months, with their softneck cousins lasting up to 12 months. Of course, there are always a few things to remember to help increase the durability of stored bulbs so you can enjoy your homegrown cloves for as long as possible.

Taking the proper care during the drying stage will prepare the garlic bulbs for winter storage. Keep the heads of garlic intact for as long as possible and always use damaged or split bulbs first. Fresh garlic is stored best when kept in dry, dark places. Bulbs keep extraordinarily well in cool temperatures (50 to 55°F/10 to 12°C).

Long-Term Storage

A basement or cold room is ideal for long-term storage (6 to 12 months). Garlic can be kept in mesh bags, baskets, or even cardboard boxes with slits to allow for proper ventilation. Place the bulbs in containers in thin layers, avoiding too much weight that may bruise the bulbs.

Never place fresh bulbs in plastic bags or containers. Garlic needs to breathe. Storing in plastic creates an anaerobic environment that will not only spoil the bulbs but can also enable *Clostridium botulinum* (the bacteria responsible for causing botulism) to breed.

Short-Term Storage

For shorter storage in the kitchen (one to three months), a cool cupboard will often be sufficient. There are also many styles of garlic keepers: ceramic containers with holes in the side for airflow. Look to a local artisan market to find the perfect one for a shady corner on the countertop. Fresh bulbs won't keep forever this way, but they'll stay fresh long enough for you to cook with.

Avoid placing garlic in the fridge. The low temperature and dark atmosphere mimic its planting conditions. Refrigerated bulbs will likely sprout early in the season, their shoots triggered by the exact environment necessary for vernalization.

What to Do If Garlic Starts to Sprout

If by chance tiny green sprouts come out of your garlic cloves, don't panic. It is actually a very good thing. The sprouts serve as a reminder that your garlic is healthy and doing exactly what it is meant to do— grow! But it is also a sign that the bulbs may not last much longer. You can still consume cloves that show signs of growing. Some people find the shoots to taste somewhat bitter, but they are edible. You may also choose to simply remove the green bits before adding the garlic to your favorite recipes.

It's a good idea to inspect your stored garlic bulbs regularly throughout winter. Watch for soft or sprouting bulbs. Remove any that have begun to spoil and use them right away, if you can. To further extend your garlic crop, consider using alternative preservation methods. Creating homemade garlic powders or freezing minced garlic can help extend the shelf life of your harvest (see page 212).

Preserving Garlic

While you can simply store garlic bulbs whole, you can also extend the harvest by preserving them for use in the kitchen, ensuring your family can eat this locally grown produce year-round. Many gardeners spend their summers preserving fresh vegetables into pickles, jams, or jellies. In the case of garlic, the easiest preserving methods involve dehydrating and freezing rather than canning.

How to Make Dehydrated Garlic Powder

Dehydrating garlic for later use in the form of garlic powder or granulated garlic is a perfect way to provide a homegrown source of garlic for those times when fresh bulbs are not an option.

To begin, separate the garlic bulbs and peel the cloves. Thinly slice the cloves or use a food processor to coarsely chop the garlic. Spread the garlic on dehydrator sheets in thin layers and dry in a food dehydrator at 120°F (49°C) until completely dry. Let cool, then transfer the pieces to a spice grinder or clean coffee grinder. Pulse until the desired texture is reached. Sift the powder through a fine-mesh strainer to catch any large pieces. Return the large pieces to the grinder, or store them separately to use as dehydrated granulated garlic in cooking.

NOTE: One-half teaspoon of garlic powder is equivalent to four garlic cloves. You will probably notice that your homemade garlic powder is quite a bit stronger than store-bought, so a little goes a long way!

How to Freeze Garlic

Freezing minced garlic is a great way to lengthen the journey of a bountiful crop. Separate the garlic bulbs and peel the cloves. Mince the garlic in a food processor or a garlic press. Form the minced garlic into 1-inch cubes; depending on the size of the cloves, two or three minced cloves will make one cube. Place the cubes on a cookie sheet lined with waxed paper. Freeze the cubes until completely solid, then transfer to an airtight freezer bag and store for up to six months in the freezer. Take out a cube when needed and add it directly to the recipe.

CREATIVE STORAGE METHODS

Depending on the size of your harvest, you may be interested in using more traditional methods to store fresh garlic bulbs. For centuries garlic braids have decorated kitchens and cold rooms. Their beauty and functionality have made them quite popular again in recent years. Hardneck garlic is challenging to braid, but there are a few tricks to help achieve the same effect as with softneck garlic (see page 154). Hand-tied garlic bouquets are a wonderful alternative to a braid, and I love being able to work in natural elements with foraged grasses or bright flowers grown in the garden (see page 156).

Acknowledgments

I OWE EVERYTHING to my parents. When I said I wanted to learn as much as I could about farming and how to operate the equipment, they showed me how. When I wanted to quit my job, they gave their unwavering support. When my business expanded and I needed help, they willingly offered their time. My mom planted my first garden with me and nurtured within me a love for home-cooked meals using fresh ingredients. My dad is one of the hardest-working men I have ever known. He sleeps when it is all done, and still somehow has time to help me in my pursuit of farming. His example of a work ethic is one that I can only hope to match someday. We work well together, with him always pushing me to be better. The Graves family farm is rich in history . . . one that is not even close to being finished.

The Graves family farm is rich in history . . . one that is not even close to being finished.

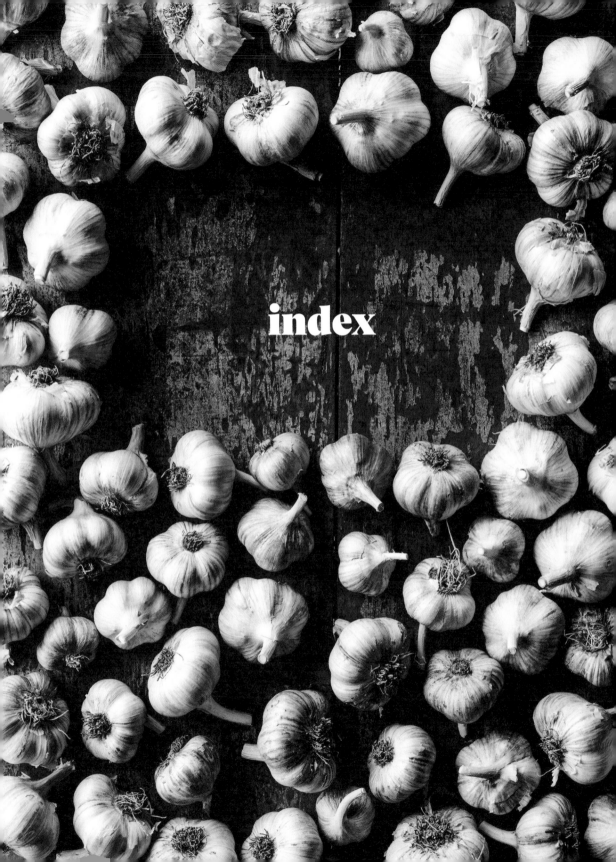

index

Page numbers in *italics* indicate photos.

e

edible flowers. *See* flowers, edible
eggs
  Breakfast Toast, Black Garlic, *90*, 91
elephant garlic, 28, *29*

f

fall
  garlic-themed dinner, 126–27
  growing garlic and, 166–67
  planting garlic in, 179–180
  recipes for, 38
farmers' markets, 30
flavor of garlic
  evolving for flavor, 16, 18
  fresh garlic, 174
  layers of, 35
Flower Arrangements, Scape and Mixed,
  129, 130, *131*
flowers, edible
  Beer-Battered Zucchini Blossoms with
    Garlic Scape Filling, *70*, 71–72, *73*
  Butter Board, Festive, *132*, 133
  Cheeseball, Roasted Garlic and
    Nasturtium, *56*, 57
  Garlic Flowers, Roasted, 82, *83*
folklore, garlic in, 18
foodborne illness, garlic and, 21
freezing garlic scapes, 199
freezing minced garlic, 212
fresh garlic, 42–53
  Beef, Garlic Ginger, 52, *53*
  Bread, Herbed Garlic, 47, *47*
  Confit, Garlic, 43, *43*
  flavor and, 174
  Pizza, Garlic Confit Flatbread, *44*, 45
  Ribs, Honey Garlic, *50*, 51
  Soup, Immune Booster, 48, *49*

g

garlic bulbil(s)
  garlic plant and, 164
  harvesting, 196
  propagation using, 178
garlic bulbs. *See also* decor, dried bulbs
  as; harvesting garlic bulbs
  Centerpiece, Illuminated Garlic, 140, *141*
  cracking, planting and, 185, *185*
  garlic plant and, 164, *165*
  Place Settings, Garlic Bulb, 134, *135*
  size matters, 209, *209*
  Table Runner, Garlic, Herb, and
    Sunflower, 136–39, *137*, *138*, *139*
garlic cloves
  depth of, planting and, 186
  peeling, 46
garlic club, 33
garlic festivals, 30–32
Garlic Flowers, Roasted, 82, *83*
garlic gatherings, 122
  celebrations at the farm, 143
  crafts for, 121
garlic plant, 164, *165*. *See also* specific
  part
garlic powder, 108
  Cabbage Slaw, Grandma's Garlic, 114, *115*
  Cookies, Savory Shortbread, *112*, 113
  making dehydrated, 212
  Salt, Rosemary Garlic, 110, *111*
garlic scape powder
  Croutons, Garlic Scape, 118, *119*
  Popcorn, Rosemary–Garlic Scape, *116*,
    117
garlic scapes, 62
  Beer-Battered Zucchini Blossoms with
    Garlic Scape Filling, *70*, 71–72, *73*
  Butter, Mint and Garlic Scape, 64, *65*
  Cornbread Muffins, Garlic Scape, 74, *75*
  Croutons, Garlic Scape, 119
  Crown, Garlic Scape, *144*, 145
  dehydrating, 199

Metric Conversion Charts

WEIGHT

TO CONVERT	TO	MULTIPLY
ounces	grams	ounces by 28.35
pounds	grams	pounds by 453.5
pounds	kilograms	pounds by 0.45

VOLUME

TO CONVERT	TO	MULTIPLY
teaspoons	milliliters	teaspoons by 4.93
tablespoons	milliliters	tablespoons by 14.79
fluid ounces	milliliters	fluid ounces by 29.57
cups	milliliters	cups by 236.59
cups	liters	cups by 0.24
pints	milliliters	pints by 473.18
pints	liters	pints by 0.473
quarts	milliliters	quarts by 946.36
quarts	liters	quarts by 0.946
gallons	liters	gallons by 3.785

LENGTH

TO CONVERT	TO	MULTIPLY
inches	centimeters	inches by 2.54
feet	meters	feet by 0.3048
yards	meters	yards by 0.9144
miles	kilometers	miles by 1.609344